# A Course of Experiments with He-Ne Laser

## SECOND EDITION

**R.S. SIROHI**
M.Sc., Ph.D. (Physics)
Professor
Department of Physics
Indian Institute of Technology
Chennai

PUBLISHING FOR ONE WORLD
**NEW AGE INTERNATIONAL (P) LIMITED, PUBLISHERS**
New Delhi • Bangalore • Chennai • Cochin • Guwahati • Hyderabad
Jalandhar • Kolkata • Lucknow • Mumbai • Ranchi
Visit us at **www.newagepublishers.com**

Published by New Age International (P) Ltd., Publishers
First Edition: 1989
Second Edition: 1991
Reprint: 2009

---



***Branches:***
- 36, Malikarjuna Temple Street, Opp. ICWA, Basavanagudi, **Bangalore**. © (080) 26677815
- 26, Damodaran Street, T. Nagar, **Chennai**. © (044) 24353401
- Hemsen Complex, Mohd. Shah Road, Paltan Bazar, Near Starline Hotel, **Guwahati**. © (0361) 2543669
- No. 105, 1st Floor, Madhiray Kaveri Tower, 3-2-19, Azam Jahi Road, Nimboliadda, **Hyderabad**. © (040) 24652456
- RDB Chambers (Formerly Lotus Cinema) 106A,1st Floor, S.N. Banerjee Road, **Kolkata**. © (033) 22275247
- 18, Madan Mohan Malviya Marg, **Lucknow**. © (0522) 2209578
- 142C, Victor House, Ground Floor, N.M. Joshi Marg, Lower Parel, **Mumbai**. © (022) 24927869
- 22, Golden House, Daryaganj, **New Delhi**. © (011) 23262370, 23262368

---

**ISBN: 978-81-224- 0311-4**

**Rs. 120.00**

**C-09-01-3317**

Printed in India at Glorious Printers, Delhi.

**PUBLISHING FOR ONE WORLD**
**NEW AGE INTERNATIONAL (P) LIMITED, PUBLISHERS**
4835/24, Ansari Road, Daryaganj, New Delhi-110002
Visit us at **www.newagepublishers.com**

# Preface to the Second Edition

The second edition includes some additional experiments. A procedure to measure divergence, beam waist and its location simultaneously has been included. An accurate method to measure the focal length of a positive lens using diffraction at a grating is described. Another experiment includes some concepts of resolving power of a lens.

The second edition is rewritten and errors in the first edition have been removed.

January 1991 R.S. SIROHI

# Preface to the First Edition

Often a question has been asked 'What do I do with the He-Ne laser'? This book attempts to answer this question. There are a number of experiments that can be done with the quasi-monochromatic light. This is particularly so for the experiments discussed under interference, diffraction and polarisation. What seems to be difficult to observe with quasi-monochromatic light, can be projected with a laser beam and the visual experience can be shared by a larger audience. In my opinion the experiments on diffraction should be demonstrated to the students to make them understand the importance of diffraction in image formation. It will be delightful to observe the diffraction pattern of a pin-hole projected on the screen.

Initially the basic concepts in filtering, holography and speckles were varified by skillfully conducted experiments with quasi-monochromatic light. These experiments now can be done with the ease using laser radiation. The concepts in holography can be best understood by recording an efficient hologram and reconstructing the object field. The experiments reported here bring out the importance of holography in the measurement area. Similarly the experiments using speckle phenomenon are in the measurement area and can be easily performed in any under graduate laboratory. Some of the abstract concepts in image formation are beautifully demonstrated by a few experiments using spatial filtering. The measurement of flow velocities can be done by measuring the Doppler frequency. A very simple experiment in flow measurement demonstrates essential features of a LDA (Laser Doppler Anemometer).

The book is an attempt to expose the students to some simple experiments; it does not exhaust the possibilities of using He-Ne laser. It is hoped that it would be useful to students in Science and Engineering.

I am thankful to Sri Kehar Singh, Professor, IIT Delhi for his valuable comments and suggestions. I also acknowledge the help rendered by my colleagues in the Engineering Design Centre.

R.S. Sirohi

# List of Experiments

# Contents

# Introduction to He-Ne Laser

Laser is a device which amplifies or generates radiation by means of the stimulated emission process. Its name is derived from the initials of Light Amplification by Stimulated Emission of Radiation. All lasers require an active medium for amplification in a narrow frequency region by population inversion achieved between a pair of energy levels. Under the conditions of population inversion, the amplification of a wave will occur as it passes through the active medium. This amplification is coherent, i.e., the phase of the wave is preserved as it traverses through the medium.

The He-Ne laser is the most widely used laser with continuous power output in the range of a fraction of mW to tens of mW. It is relatively easy to construct

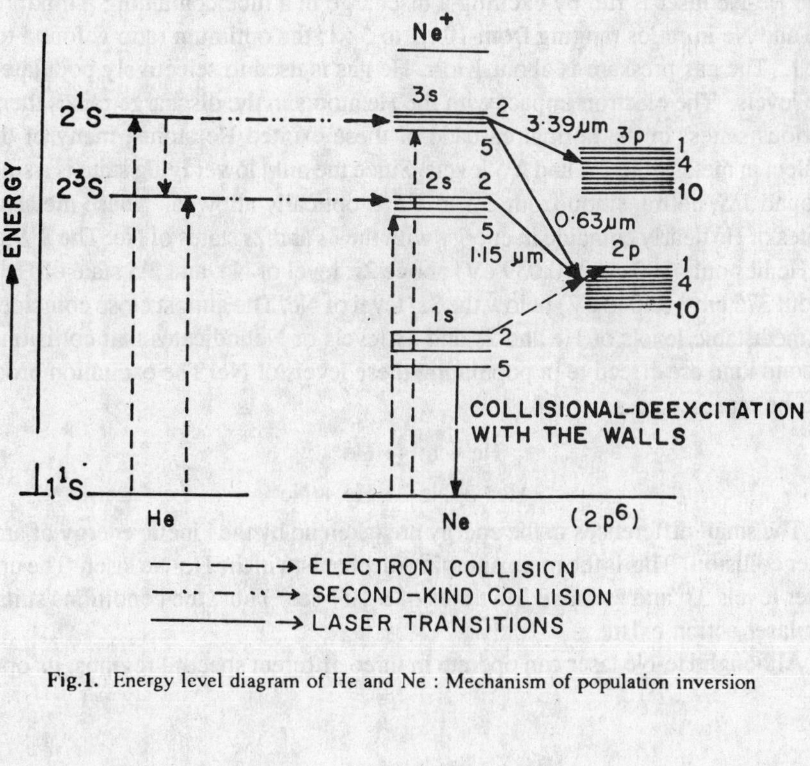


**Fig.1.** Energy level diagram of He and Ne : Mechanism of population inversion

and is reliable in operation. The laser transitions occur in neutral Ne atom, and He plays the role of selectively populating the pertinent energy states of Ne so as to produce population inversion. There are three principal transitions at 0.6328 μm, 1.15 μm and 3.39 μm. The He-Ne laser has, however, been operated to lase at discrete frequencies in the whole visible region. The energy level diagrams of He and Ne are shown in Fig. 1. Energy level diagram of Ne is represented by Paschen notation and of He by Russel-Saunders (R-S) notation. R-S terminology using L-S coupling is not a particularly good description of the Ne system because the transitions eptly observed would correspond to forbidden transitions.

The Ne states in Fig. 1 correspond to the following electron configurations:

| State | Electron configuration | No. of levels |
|---|---|---|
| Ground | $2p^6$ | 1 |
| $1s_{2\text{-}5}$ | $2p^5 3s$ | 4 |
| $2p_{1\text{-}10}$ | $2p^5 3p$ | 10 |
| $2s_{2\text{-}5}$ | $2p^5 4s$ | 4 |
| $3p_{1\text{-}10}$ | $2p^5 4p$ | 10 |
| $3s_{2\text{-}5}$ | $2p^5 5s$ | 4 |

## Mechanism of Population Invers'on

The He-Ne laser is run by exciting a discharge in a tube containing a mixture of He and Ne in ratios ranging from 10 : 1 to 5 : 1; the optimum ratio is found to be 7 : 1. The gas pressure is about 1 torr. He gas is used to selectively populate the Ne levels. The electron impact with the He atoms in the discharge raises them to various states. In the normal cascade of these excited He atoms, many of them collect in metastable $2^1S$ and $2^3S$ levels. Since the only lower lying state is a singlet ground $1^1S$, no transition from $2^3S$ to $1^1S$ is optically allowed. These metastable states of He nearly coincide in energy with the $3s$ and $2s$ states of Ne. The $2^3S$ state of He lies only 300 cm$^{-1}$ (0.039 eV) above $2s_2$ level of Ne, and $2^1S$ state of He lies about 375 cm$^{-1}$ (0.048 eV) below the $3s_2$ level of Ne. The almost close coincidence of metastable levels of He and $2s$ and $3s$ levels of Ne indicates that collisions of second kind are effective in populating these levels of Ne. The excitation process can be represented as

$$\text{He} + e^- \rightarrow \text{He}^*$$

$$\text{He}^* + \text{Ne} \rightarrow \text{He} + \text{Ne}^*$$

The small differences in the energy are taken up by the kinetic energy of atoms after collision. This is the main pumping mechanism in the He-Ne laser. The upper laser levels $3s$ and $2s$ have life times of $\simeq 10^{-8}$ sec. Thus, the conditions suitable for laser action exist.

Although He-Ne laser can operate in three different spectral regions, its operation in red at 0.6328 μm is usually expected when it is to be used for alignment, interferometry, data processing, holography etc. The visible He-Ne laser radiation at 0.6328 μm arises from the $3s_2$ to $2p_4$ transition. The terminal $2p$ group of levels decays radiatively with a life time of about $10^{-8}$ sec. to the long lived $1s$ state. Because of the long life of $1s$ state, atoms in this state tend to collect with time. These atoms collide with electrons in the discharge and are excited back into the lower laser level $2p_4$, which thus reduces the inversion and can even quench it. To avoid this, the atoms in $1s$ state are brought to ground state by collisional de-excitation with the walls of the tube. For this reason, the gain in 0.6328 μm transition is found to increase with decreasing tube diameters. Further the gain depends on the pressure of the gas. The optimum gain is obtained when the product of pressure and tube diameter is in the range of 2.9-3.66 torr-mm. The gain at 0.6328 μm does not increase linearly with the length of the tube as expected. The reason for this is that the high gain at 3.39 μm results in super radiant operation if the length is sufficiently long. This starts to drain off the upper level population of 0.6328 μm transition. This 'gain coupling' can even quench the operation at this wavelength. For this reason, dispersive elements to suppress gain at 3.39 μm are used when high power operation at 0.6328 μm is desired.

The output of He-Ne laser shows a strong dependence on the discharge current. The power supplies are, therefore, matched with the tube. It is now possible to mass produce laser tubes with reproducible characteristics, and hence compatible power supply unit can be used for the operation.

Figure 2 shows a schematic of a He-Ne laser. The laser consists of a laser head and a power supply. The laser head is either an internal mirrors (Fig. 2a) or an

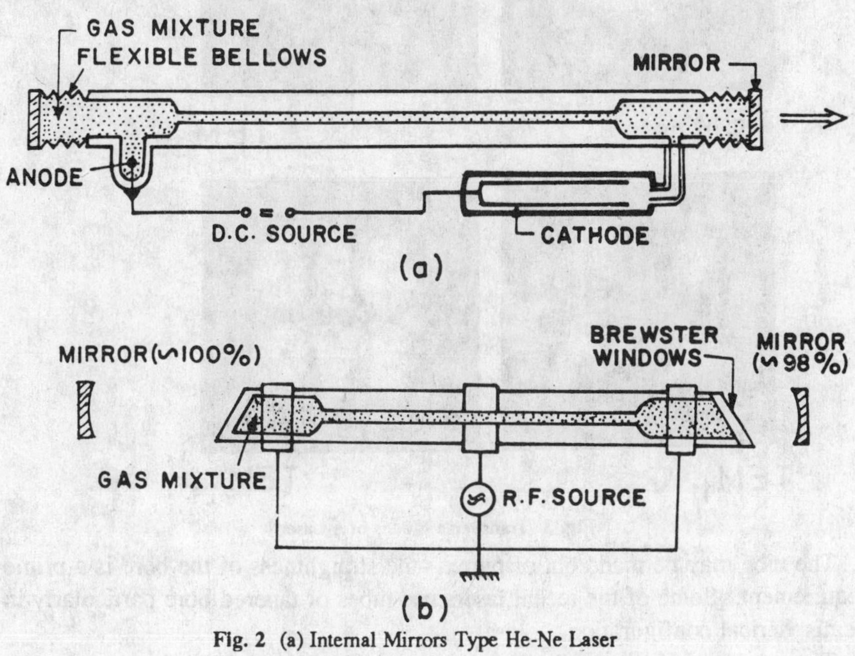


Fig. 2 (a) Internal Mirrors Type He-Ne Laser
(b) External Mirrors Type He-Ne Laser

external mirrors configuration (Fig. 2b). The small lasers are usually of internal mirrors type, wherein the mirrors are permanently sealed at the end of the tube. The laser tube is prealigned, and it remains aligned during transit and operation. Some of these lasers have step bore capillaries to suppress higher transverse modes and provide optimum power output. The laser output is randomly polarized.

In an external mirrors laser head, the Brewster windows are attached at the ends of the tube to contain the gas mixture. The Brewster windows have 100% transmittance (excluding very small absorption and scattering losses) for the *p*-polarized component thereby providing linearly polarized output. The orientation of the linearly polarized beam can be varied either by rotating the tube in the housing or the laser itself. The mirrors are mounted on an invar structure to keep the cavity length constant, and are provided with alignment screws. This arrangement is flexible and higher order transverse modes can be supported by proper alignment of the mirrors. Usually the laser will oscillate in multi-modes, particularly so when the power is to be maximized. By introducing loss by misalignment, the laser is made to oscillate in the fundamental $TEM_{00}$ mode. Figure 3 shows a photograph of some of the trnasverse modes which can be observed by manipulating the screws on the mirrors.

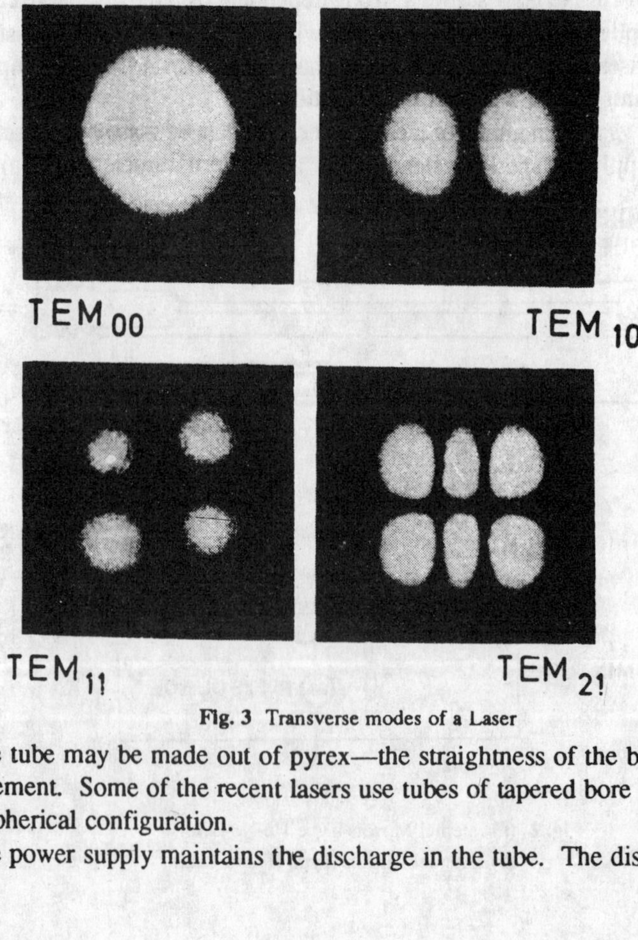


**Fig. 3** Transverse modes of a Laser

The tube may be made out of pyrex—the straightness of the bore is a prime requirement. Some of the recent lasers use tubes of tapered bore particularly in hemispherical configuration.

The power supply maintains the discharge in the tube. The discharge can be maintained by a d.c. source or an r.f. source. A ballast resistance to control the current in the laser is mounted very near to the anode. All laser supplies are high voltage supplies and care should be exercised while using the lasers.

The tube containing He-Ne gas mixture is placed between a pair of mirrors: One mirror is completely reflecting (99.99% reflectivity) and the other mirror, called the output mirror, is partially transmitting. The mirrors constitute a cavity or a resonator. In a Fabry-Perot resonator both the mirrors are plane. If one of the mirrors is flat and other has a radius of curvature equal to the mirrors separation, a hemispherical resonator results. One can indeed conceive large number of resonator configurations, some of them are stable. The He-Ne lasers use stable resonator configurations. Some of the well-known configurations are shown in Fig. 4.

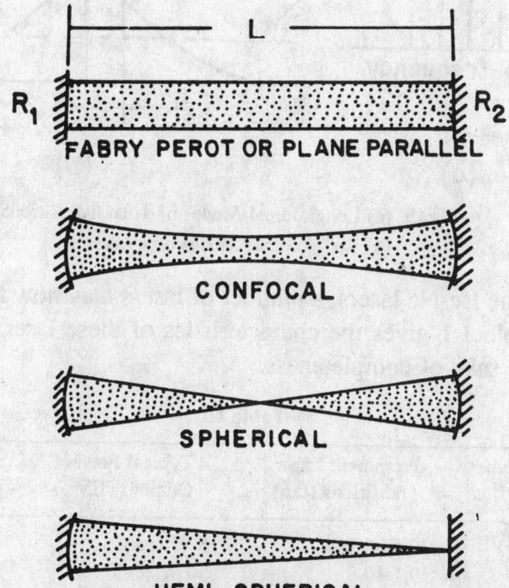


**Fig. 4.** Resonator Configurations

A beam bounces back and forth between the mirrors. If the population inversion between two levels has been established, and the gain is more than the losses in the cavity, a laser beam is produced. A mode of a resonator can be defined as a self-consistent field configuration, i.e., the optical field distribution reproduces itself after one round trip in the resonator. The modes of a resonator are transverse electromagnetic waves with definite transverse irradiance distributions. A mode pattern is characterized by two integers, i.e., $m$ and $n$ (thus $TEM_{mn}$ mode), which are the number of zeros in the field along $x$ and $y$ directions. A $TEM_{00}$ mode is the fundamental mode and has least diffraction loss. The irradiance distribution of $TEM_{00}$ mode is gaussian in any cross-section of the beam. The laser usually can be made to work in $TEM_{00}$ mode.

A passive plane parallel mirrors configuration can support infinitely large longitudinal modes that are separated by $c/2L$, where $c$ is the velocity of light and $L$ is the mirrors separation. When the gain medium is enclosed, only those modes that lie within the line profile and have sufficient gain will be supported as shown in Fig. 5. The output of the laser may, therefore, consist of a number of longitudinal modes separated by $c/2L$. If the laser cavity is very small, say about 14 cm long, only one longitudinal mode is supported, and the output of the laser would be of a single frequency. The frequency may, however, wander in the gain curve. The frequency of the laser can be stabilized by keeping the cavity length constant. The temporal coherence of the laser is then extremely long.

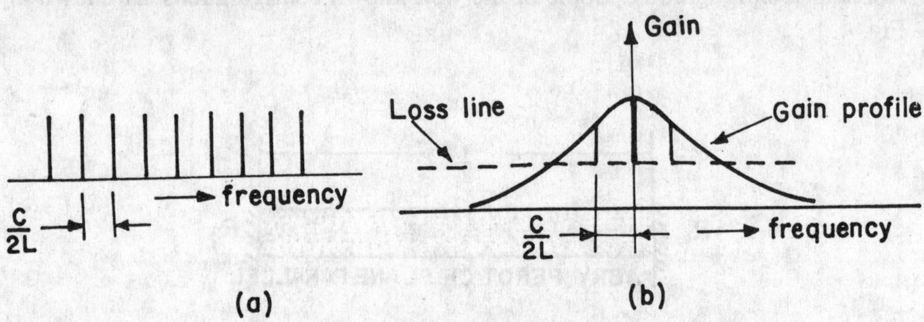


**Fig. 5** (a) Longitudinal Modes of a Passive Resonator
(b) Longitudinal Modes of a Laser

Apart from the He-Ne lasers, a number of lasers may now be available in the Laboratory. Table 1.1 gives the characteristics of these lasers. He-Ne laser is included for the sake of completeness.

**Table 1.1**

| Sl. No. | Laser Type | Prominent Laser Transitions (μm) | Typical Power Output ($TEM_{00}$) | Remarks |
|---|---|---|---|---|
| 1. | Argon Ion | 0.45-0.514 | 5 W (cw) | CW |
| 2. | $CO_2$ | 9.1-10.8 | 50 W (cw) | can be pulsed |
| 3. | Cu-Vapour | 0.511, 0.578 | 20-30 W (multimode) | |
| 4. | He-Cd | 0.325, 0.442 | 3 mW, 30 mW(cw) | |
| 5. | He-Ne | 0.6328 | 0.5-80 mW(cw) | |
| 6. | Krypton Ion | 0.33-0.8 | 3.5 W (cw) | |
| 7. | Nd:Yag | 1.06 | 4 W (cw) | |
| | | 0.53 | 1 W (cw) | |
| | | 1.06 | 10 J | pulsed |
| | | 0.53 | 1 J | pulsed |
| 8. | Ruby | 0.694 | 10 J | pulsed |
| 9. | Semiconductor | 0.78 | 3mW (cw) | drive 30 mA |
| | | 0.815 | 3 mW (cw) | 30 mA |
| | | 0.82 | 1 mW (cm) | 300 mA |
| | | 0.84 | 3 mW (cw) | 20 mA |
| | | 0.85 | 4 mW (cw) | 90 mA |

# 1. Laser Beam Parameters

## 1.1 Power Distribution within the Beam

Power distribution within the beam can be studied by a number of techniques, viz., photographic technique, scanning technique, etc. We shall, however, discuss a method which is very simple to perform in the laboratory. Further the spot-size and the divergence of the beam can also be measured with this method. The method involves the measurement of the power past a knife-edge which is slowly inserted in the beam. In order to understand the principle of the method, let us assume that the laser is oscillating in $TEM_{00}$ mode so that the spatial distribution of the beam is gaussian. Let $P_0$ be the total power in the beam of spot size $2w_0$. The irradiance distribution $I(x,y)$ as a function of the cartesian coordinates $(x,y)$ measured from the beam center perpendicular to the direction of propagation is given by

$$I\,(x,y) = \frac{2P_0}{\pi w_0^2}\ \exp\left(-\frac{2(x^2+y^2)}{w_0^2}\right) \tag{1.1}$$

The power $P$ transmitted past a knife-edge blocking off all points for which $x \leq a$ is, therefore, given by

$$P = \int_{-\infty}^{\infty}\int_{a}^{\infty} I\,(x,y)\,dx\,dy = \frac{P_0}{2}\ \mathrm{erfc}\left(\frac{a\sqrt{2}}{w_0}\right) \tag{1.2}$$

where $a$ is the depth of knife-edge in the beam and erfc($x$) is the complementary error function. Therefore, the integrated power past the knife-edge inserted in a gaussian beam is given by the complementary error function. For other spatial distributions, an integrated power curve can be obtained from which the power distribution in the beam can be realised. It may be noted that this method uses information from all the points of the irradiance distribution in the beam unlike scanning technique.

**Experiment 1.1:** Determination of the power distribution within the beam.

**Equipments:** A gas laser, a knife-edge mounted on a micropositioner, a photodetector of a large linear range, a lens, a bench.

**Procedure:** The schematic of the experimental set-up is shown Fig. 1.1. The knife-edge is mounted normal to the beam at any desired plane. A lens is used to focus the laser beam past the knife-edge on the photo-detector. The lens is of sufficiently large aperture as to gather all the diffracted light and is placed close to the knife-edge. An interference filter is mounted in front of the detector. The experiment can be conducted in a relatively well lit room now.

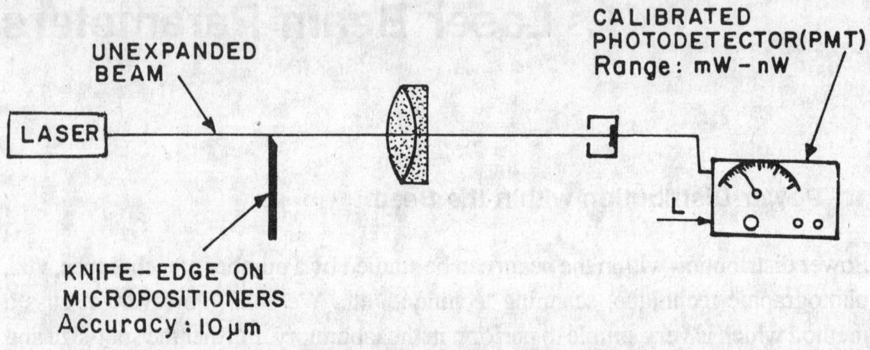


Fig. 1.1 Study of Power Distribution in the Beam

The knife-edge is manually inserted in the beam and corresponding output of the detector is noted. The output of the detector is plotted as a function of the position of the knife-edge. This gives a curve which represents one-dimensional integrated power distribution. Fig. 1.2 shows such a curve when the knife-edge is (i) inserted and (ii) withdrawn in the beam.

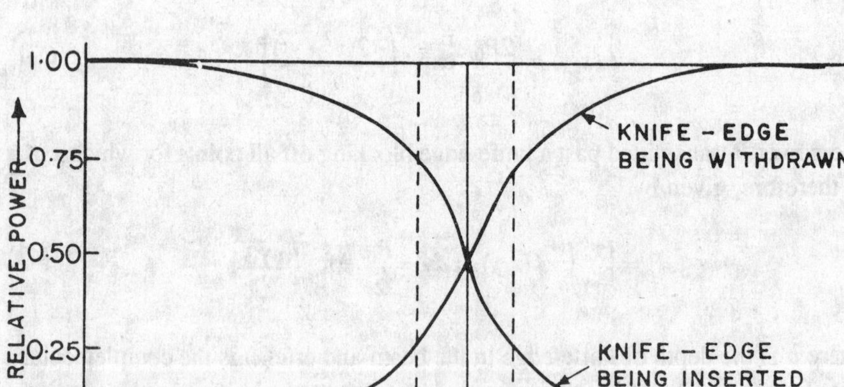


Fig. 1.2 Plot of Relative Power vs Knife-Edge Position

Alternatively the knife-edge is mounted on a motorized stage and the output of the photo-detector is connected to a recorder. The curve for one-dimensional integrated power distribution can be then plotted in a straight forward way.

The irradiance distribution in the beam can be constructed from the integrated power distribution curve. The power distribution in the beam can also be obtained by directly placing a linear diode array; the output of each diode is proportional to the intensity incident on it.

## 1.2 Spot Size of the Beam

Consider the irradiance distribution represented by Eq.(1.1): $w_0$ is the radius at which irradiance falls to $e^{-2}$ times its central value. $2w_0$ is, therefore, taken as the spot size.

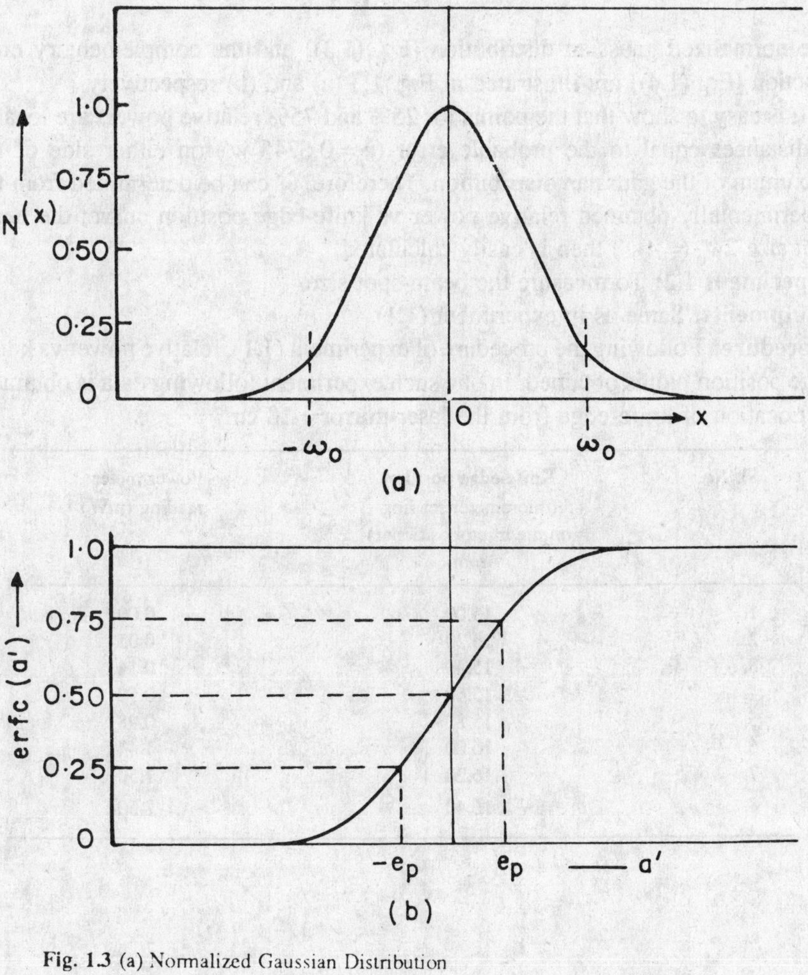


Fig. 1.3 (a) Normalized Gaussian Distribution

(b) Relative Power Distribution as a Function of Knife-Edge Position

A gaussian beam remains gaussian as it propagates in vacuum or in a homogeneous medium. The output of a laser oscillating in $TEM_{00}$ mode is gaussian, and the spot size $2w_0$ refers to the planer wavefront. At any other plane the wavefront will be either converging or diverging and will have spot size larger than $2w_0$. It is meaningful to measure the spot size for a gaussian beam only. Eq. (1.1) can be cast into a well-known normalized gaussian distribution by setting $w_0 = 2w'$, as

$$\frac{I(x, y)}{P_0} = \frac{1}{2\pi w'^2} \exp\left\{-\frac{(x^2+y^2)}{2w'^2}\right\} \tag{1.3}$$

where w' is the standard deviation.

Similarly, Eq. (1.2) can be written as

$$\frac{P}{P_0} = \frac{1}{2} \operatorname{erfc}\left(\frac{a}{\sqrt{2}w'}\right) \tag{1.4}$$

The normalized gaussian distribution [Eq. (1.3)] and the complementary error function [Eq. (1.4)] are illustrated in Fig. 1.3 (a) and (b) respectively.

It is easy to show that the points for 25% and 75% relative powers are located at distances equal to the probable error ($e_p = 0.6745\ w'$) on either side of the maximum of the gaussian distribution. Therefore, $w'$ can be determined from the experimentally obtained relative power vs knife-edge position curve; the beam spot size $2w_0$ ($= 4w'$) then is easily calculated.

**Experiment 1.2:** To measure the beam-spot size.

**Equipments:** Same as in experiment (1.1).

**Procedure:** Following the procedure of experiment (1.1), relative power vs knife-edge position plot is obtained. In one such experiment following data is obtained:

Location of knife-edge from the laser mirror = 10 cm

| Sl. No. | Knife-edge position (micrometer reading on the micropositioner) mm | Power meter reading (mW) |
|---|---|---|
| 1. | 15.00 | 0.00 |
| 2. | 15.20 | 0.03 |
| 3. | 15.40 | 0.14 |
| 4. | 15.60 | 0.50 |
| 5. | 15.80 | 0.98 |
| 6. | 16.00 | 1.44 |
| 7. | 16.20 | 1.50 |
| 8. | 16.40 | 1.50 |

A graph between position and power meter reading is plotted as in Fig. 1.4.

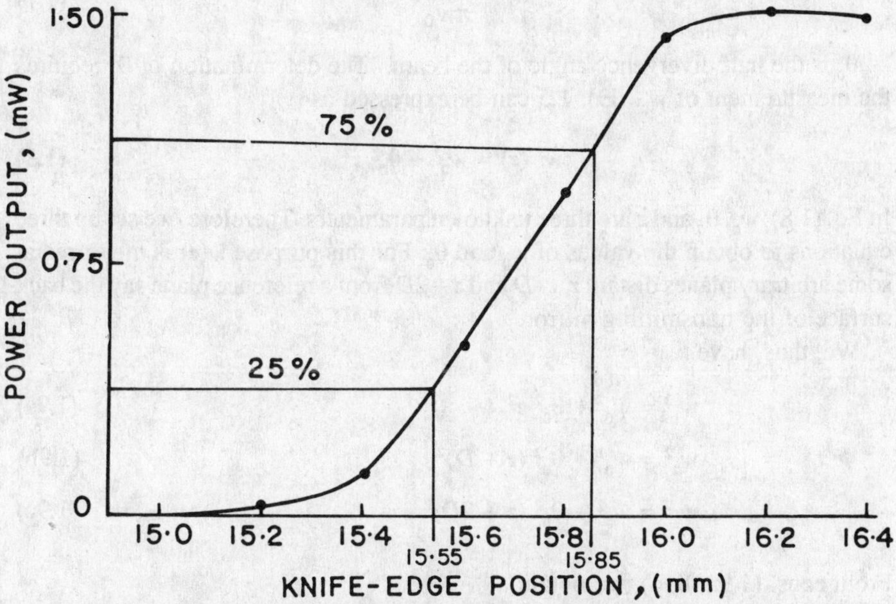


**Fig. 1.4** Plot of Power Output vs Knife-Edge Position

From the graph, it is found that the positions corresponding to 25% and 75% power outputs are 15.55 mm and 15.85 mm respectively. This gives a probable error of 0.15 mm. Therefore, $w' = 0.15/0.6745 = 0.22$ mm. The beam spot size at a plane 10 cm from the laser output mirror is thus $4 \times 0.22 = 0.88$ mm.

## 1.3 Divergence of the Laser Beam

We shall again assume that the laser is oscillating in $TEM_{00}$ mode; its output is a gaussian beam. The gaussian beam has the least divergence and maximum power contained in the prescribed area of the beam. It can be shown that the radius $w(z)$ of the beam varies with $z$(taken along the direction of propagation) as

$$w(z) = w_0 \left[ 1 + \left( \frac{\lambda z}{\pi w_0^2} \right)^2 \right]^{1/2} \tag{1.5}$$

where $2w_0$ is the waist diameter (diameter where the wavefront is plane) of the beam and $\lambda$ is the wavelength of laser radiation.

The gradient $\dfrac{dw(z)}{dz}$ [= $\theta(z)$] of the beam radius locus at a distance $z$ is given by

$$\theta(z) = \left( \frac{\lambda}{\pi w_0} \right)^2 \frac{z}{w_0} \left[ 1 + \left( \frac{\lambda z}{\pi w_0^2} \right)^2 \right]^{-1/2} \tag{1.6}$$

The angle $\theta(z)$ varies with $z$. However, when $z \to \infty$, $\theta(z) = \theta(\infty) \to \theta_0$, where

$$\theta_0 = \frac{\lambda}{\pi w_0} \tag{1.7}$$

$\theta_0$ is the half divergence angle of the beam. The determination of $\theta_0$ requires the measurement of $w_0$. Eq. 1.5 can be expressed as

$$w^2(z) = w_0^2 + \theta_0^2 z^2 \tag{1.8}$$

In Eq. (1.8) $w_0$, $\theta_0$ and $z$ are three unknown parameters. Therefore, we set up three equations to obtain the values of $w_0$ and $\theta_0$. For this purpose $w(z)$ is measured at some arbitrary planes distant $z$, $z+D$ and $z + 2D$ from a reference plane say the back surface of the transmitting mirror.

We, thus, have

$$w_1^2 = w_0^2 + \theta_0^2 z^2 \tag{1.9a}$$

$$w_2^2 = w_0^2 + \theta_0^2 (z + D)^2 \tag{1.9b}$$

$$w_3^2 = w_0^2 + \theta_0^2 (z + 2D)^2 \tag{1.9c}$$

From eqns. (1.9a, b, c), we obtain

$$2\theta_0^2 D^2 = w_3^2 - 2w_2^2 + w_1^2$$

$$\text{or} \quad \theta_0 = \frac{1}{\sqrt{2}D} (w_3^2 - 2w_2^2 + w_1^2)^{1/2} \tag{1.10a}$$

Thus $\theta_0$ is measured in terms of experimentally measured beam radii. Further $w_0$ is obtained from

$$w_0 = \frac{\lambda}{\pi \theta_0} \tag{1.10b}$$

The distance $z$ of the beam radii can also be calculated using the following relation

$$z = (w_1^2 - w_0^2)^{1/2}/\theta_0 \tag{1.10c}$$

Following the procedure described in experiment (1.2), the beam spot sizes are measured at three different planes at $z = z$, $z+D$ and $z+2D$ respectively. The separation $D$ is measured with a meter scale. The divergence angle is then calculated using Eq.(1.10a). The waist size $w_0$ can be calculated using Eq. (1.10b) and the location of beam radii by using Eq. (1.10c). The procedure may be repeated by measuring spot sizes at additional equi-spaced planes.

Another simple method to determine $\theta_0$ is to insert a lens of precisely known focal length $f$ in the beam and measure the radius of focal spot $w_f$. The divergence $\theta_0$ is given by

$$\theta_0 = \frac{w_f}{f} \tag{1.11}$$

**Experiment 1.3:** To measure the divergence of a laser beam.
**Equipments:** Same as in experiment 1.1.
**Procedure:** Following the procedure described in experiment (1.2), the beam spot sizes are measured at three equally spaced planes. The separation between the planes is measured with a meter scale. The divergence angle is then calculated from Eq. (1.10a) and the beam waist from Eq. (1.10b). The location of beam radii can be obtained from Eq. (1.10c). For better results, the procedure may be repeated by measuring spot sizes at additional planes and then averaging the calculated values.

## 1.4 Coherence

A sinusoidal wave exists in space for all the time and, therefore, does exhibit perfect spatial and temporal coherence. However, both perfect spatial and temporal coherence are mathematical idealisation. A real source emits waves that are limited both in time and space. The concept of spatial and temporal coherence is an involved one but it is possible to study them independently. Consider an arbitrary point source emitting spherical waves. Any two points on the spherical surface (or a plane surface at larger distance from the point source) will have fixed phase relationship and the spatial coherence exists.

A real source is a collection of a large number of point sources, and hence a real wave is a superposition of large number of spherical waves with proper phases. This decreases the area of spatial coherence. The region of coherence can be calculated using van Cittert-Zernike theorem. The spatial coherence arises due to the finite size of the source. A wave is said to exhibit perfect spatial coherence if the phase difference between two fixed points on a plane normal to the direction of propagation is time independent. The output wave of a laser oscillating in $TEM_{00}$ mode is spatially coherent over the beam irrespective of the size of beam, while the light from the sun is spatially coherent over a region of diameter of 0.01 mm. The spatial coherence can be demonstrated using Young's double slit experiment.

On the other hand, temporal coherence arises due to the finite bandwidth of the spectral line. A spectral line of finite bandwidth may be considered a combination of large number of monochromatic lines which on superposition reduce the temporal coherence. Due to the finite bandwidth, a wave is limited in space; it is called a wave train. It can exhibit fixed phase relationship between any two points over its length. If the path difference between the two waves derived from the same wave exceeds the length of the wave train ($\sim$ coherence length) no interference phenomenon can be observed. The coherence length is mathematically given as $\lambda_0^2/\Delta\lambda$, where $\lambda_0$ is the mean wavelength and $\Delta\lambda$ is the bandwidth. A wave is said to exhibit perfect temporal coherence if the phase difference between two fixed points along the direction of propagation is time independent. The temporal coherence can be demonstrated using Michelson interferometer.

We can now discuss the coherence characteristics of a laser beam. The spatially distributed radiators in the laser are forced to emit radiation in phase and hence a region of coherence exists. The region of coherence depends on the resonator configuration. If a resonator configuration supports only $TEM_{00}$ mode, the spatial distribution of the output is gaussian and the wavefront is uni-phase. Since the phase is constant over the whole beam, the region of coherence is approximately equal to the beam size. The spatial coherence is maintained over the whole beam even after beam expansion. The spatial coherence naturally is poor when the laser oscillates in multi-transverse modes.

A resonator can also support a large number of longitudinal modes. It can be shown that a passive Fabry-Perot resonator can support an infinite number of longitudinal modes. These modes are separated by $c/2L$ in frequency where $c$ is the velocity of light and $L$ is the resonator length. In the presence of gain medium, only those modes which lie in the spectral profile and have sufficient gain can be supported for the oscillation to grow. The spectral profile in He-Ne laser is Doppler broadened and hence is gaussian. It has a width of 1700 MHz. If the length of the resonator is less than 14 cm, only one of the longitudinal modes can be supported in the gain curve. This is a single frequency laser, but its frequency can vary within the gain curve due to changes in resonator length by temperature variations. A frequency stabilized laser is obtained by restricting the span of frequency in the gain curve. The bandwidth of the longitudinal mode is not strictly zero but is finite. The bandwidth is governed by the losses at the mirror and in the cavity. Nevertheless it is smaller compared to the width of the Doppler line. Therefore, the coherence length of the laser beam can be very large extending upto kilometers. For this reason it becomes difficult to measure it in the laboratory using interferometric set-up. If the laser oscillates in a number of longitudinal modes, its coherence length decreases. For example, if the laser oscillates in two longitudinal modes its coherence length is approximately equal to the length of the cavity. The coherence function is oscillatory. Therefore, objects of greater depth can be holographically recorded by properly planned layout. It is essential to know the volume of coherence of the laser beam for holographic applications.

The visibility $V$ of fringes in an interference pattern when two beams of irradiances $I_1$ and $I_2$ are superposed, is given by

$$V = \frac{2\sqrt{I_1 I_2}}{I_1 + I_2} |\gamma_{12}(\tau)|$$

where $\gamma_{12}(\tau)$ is the degree of coherence between points 1 and 2, and $\tau$ is the time delay between the two beams. If the amplitudes of the beams are equal, the visibility is equal to the absolute value of the degree of coherence. Therefore, the measurement of the fringe visibility is a direct measure of the degree of coherence.

The measurement of spatial coherence, therefore, involves studying the fringe visibility in the interference pattern as a function of the slit separation in the Young's double slit experiment.

On the other hand, the temporal coherence is measured by studying the fringe visibility as a function of path difference. The slit separation for which visibility falls from $V = 1$ to $V = 0.88$ will be take as the measure of spatial coherence. Similar definition applies to the temporal coherence. Most of the He-Ne lasers used in laboratory oscillate in $TEM_{00}$ mode and output two longitudinal modes. The measurement of both spatial and temporal coherence can, therefore, be performed in the laboratory.

**Experiment 1.4:** Demonstration of the spatial coherence of the laser beam.

**Equipments:** A gas laser, a variable double slit (or a number of double slits with different separations), a viewing screen.

**Procedure:** The experiment is usually done with the unexpanded beam that is allowed to travel sufficiently large distance so that it is of reasonable size (say about 5 mm in diameter) for the slits to insert and move. Alternatively it may be lightly expanded. The spatial coherence in the beam can be demonstrated by any one of the following procedures:

The variable double slit is inserted within the laser beam and the interference pattern is observed on a screen placed several meters away from the slit plane. The Young's fringes are straight line fringes with spacing of $\bar{x}$ $(=\lambda z/d)$ where $z$ is the separation between the slit plane and screen and $d$ is the slit separation. The fringes run parallel to the slits. The central fringe in the pattern is bright. The fringe pattern can be scanned with a photodetector carrying a tiny pin-hole. The visibility is calculated by measuring the irradiances of the central bright fringe and the minima around this. The visibility is calculated from the formula $V=(I_{max}-I_{min})/(I_{max}+I_{min})$. The visibility is measured as a function of slit separation. If the laser is oscillating in $TEM_{00}$ mode, the visibility remains practically constant for all slit separations spanning the beam. If the laser is oscillating in $TEM_{10}$ mode, the interference pattern remains stationary so long the slit pair is within one of the lobes of the beam. When the slits lie on both the lobes, the central fringe is dark; there is a shift of half fringe width when the slit pair crosses from a single lobe over to both the lobes.

The spatial coherence can also be demonstrated by scanning the laser beam with a double slit of fixed separation. It will be observed that the fringe pattern will remain stationary regardless of which portion of the beam is intercepted as long as the beam fills the double slit. This demonstrates that there is always a fixed phase relationship between the two waves from the double slit. The laser beam is thus spatially coherent across the entire beam.

**Experiment 1.5:** Demonstration of the temporal coherence of the laser beam.

**Equipments:** A gas laser, an interferometric set up (Michelson interferometer), a screen, etc.

**Procedure:** It is assumed that the laser is oscillating in $TEM_{00}$ mode so that spatial coherence exists over the whole beam. The interferometric set up (Fig. 1.5) consists of a microscope objective, a collimating lens, a beam splitter preferably wedge type, two plane mirrors (or cube corners) and a projection lens. The beam from the laser is expanded to about 25 mm in diameter using microscope objective and collimating lens combination. The collimation can be checked by a method described in Appendix B. The collimated beam is split into two beams of approximately equal irradiances by the beam splitter. The beams proceed towards

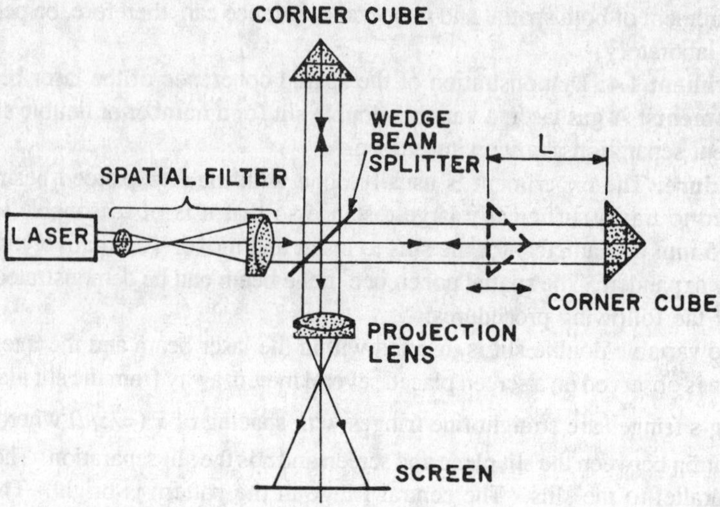


**Fig. 1.5** Demonstration of Temporal Coherence

the two plane mirrors one of which is mounted on a translatory stage. The reflected beams recombine at the beam splitter. If we place a screen at the focal plane of the projection lens, two bright spots corresponding to the two reflected beams are seen. The two spots are made coincident by adjusting the mirrors on their adjustable mounts. The interference pattern is now visible on the screen which is now placed away from the focal plane of the projection lens. The pattern contains straight line fringes whose orientation and number can be controlled by adjusting the plane mirrors.

Initially both the mirrors are kept at approximately equal distances from the beam splitting surface of the beam splitter. This corresponds to zero time delay between the two beams. The fringes of maximum contrast are, therefore, seen. The mirror on the translatory stage is now moved away parallel to itself and the visibility of the fringes as a function of path difference is studied. If the laser is oscillating in a single longitudinal mode, there is no apparent decrease in the visibility over very large distances, demonstrating a very large temporal coherence. If the laser oscillates into two longitudinal modes, the visibility would exhibit minima at the path difference which is multiple of the cavity length.

Often this exercise is done by a student prior to setting up an holographic recording arrangement. The contrast of interference pattern is observed by setting up the Michelson interferometer with unexpanded beam and moving one of the mirrors in discrete steps. The procedure described above using expanded beam and continuous motion of the mirror is obviously more accurate.

In this experiment, it should be noted that the moving mirror may tilt during traverse due to imperfect guides, and hence the interference pattern may disappear. The traverse guides on which the mirror moves should be extremely accurate. If the cube corner is substituted for the plane mirror, the interferometer becomes tilt insensitive. The long coherence length of the laser beam with cube corners as reflectors in the interferometric set up has been fully exploited in numerically controlled machines.

## 1.5 Measurement of Separation of Longitudinal Modes

It is known that the longitudinal modes are separated by $c/2L$ in frequency where $L$ is the cavity length. The mode separation can be experimentally measured. There are a number of ways of doing it. Here we mention only two of them. A Fabry-Perot etalon of approximately 100 mm length may be used. It is illuminated by a lightly divergent beam. Circular fringes belonging to each mode will be observed. Motion of these rings due to mode shift on the gain curve as the laser warms up can be observed. In the other method the laser beam falls over a photo detector say Motorola MRD500 and output of the detector is fed to a spectrum analyzer. The detector photo mixes the modes and there is an output corresponding to difference frequency. This heterodyne output can be read off on a spectrum analyzer.

### PROBLEMS

1. What is the coherence lengtn of the radiation from a mercury source that emits at the mean wavelength of 546.1 nm and line width of 0.5 Å.
2. Can we increase the coherence length of the radiation from a mercury source by using a filter? Can we do the same for the laser radiation?
3. Suggest an experimental arrangement to reduce the divergence of the laser beam by a factor of 10.
4. A laser beam of 10 mm diameter is incident on a well corrected lens of 25 mm focal length and 15 mm aperture. Calculate the power density at the focal plane of the lens. Assume that the incident beam is of 1 mW power at 632.8 nm. Discuss the result with reference to eye-hazards due to laser radiation.
5. Is it possible to perform the double slit experiment with filtered radiation from a mercury source? Can we measure the wavelength of radiation with this method?
6. Suppose each slit of the double-slit is illuminated with one of the beams from two gas lasers. Explain the nature of the pattern observable at the screen.
7. What happens when one of the slits of the double-slit is blocked? How is the irradiance distribution in the pattern?
8. Explain a method to obtain experimentally the wavelength difference between $D_1$ and $D_2$ lines of the sodium light.
9. Explain why a cube corner is insensitive to misalignment when used as a reflector in the interferometers?
10. Can we use plane parallel plate shear interferometry to study the spatial coherence of the beam?
11. Show that the points of 25% and 75% relative power in Fig. 1.3b are located at a distance of 0.6745 $w'$ from the center of the Gaussian curve.

# 2. Interference of Light

Two beams of light cross without influencing each other; their directions of propagation, amplitudes, etc. remain unchanged. But in the region of overlap, large irradiance variations occur provided the beams are coherent. This phenomenon is known as interference of light. If in the region of overlap, the irradiance at any point is either zero or minimum, it is termed as destructive interference. On the other hand, if the irradiance is maximum, it is called constructive interference.

The phenomenon of interference is observed usually with (quasi) monochromatic light. It can also be observed with white light. The bright colours seen over the thin oil layers on water, soap bubble surface, etc. are examples of this. The phenomenon of interference is observed with considerable ease provided the light is both spatially and temporally coherent. The laser is thus an obvious choice as a source.

The applications of interference phenomenon are numerous. It is used for the calibration of meter; measurement of dimensions and dimensional changes; surface testing; measurement of physical variables like refractive index, temperature, pressure, etc.; measurement of angular diameters of stellar bodies, study of weakly radiating bodies and so on. The choice of the instrument or the layout of the optical arrangement depends on the particular task at hand.

In what follows, basic principles of interference and some of the experiments that can be set up in a graduate laboratory are discussed.

## 2.1 Basic Principles

The two interfering waves should have a fixed phase relationship for the observation of a stable interference pattern. The interfering waves are, therefore, derived from the same parent wave. There are two ways to derive the interfering waves from the parent wave, namely (i) wavefront division and (ii) amplitude division.

Let $\bar{a}_1$ and $\bar{a}_2$ be the complex amplitudes of the two waves at any point on a plane. The amplitudes are expressed as

$$\bar{a}_1 = a_{10} \exp[i(wt + \bar{k}.\bar{r})], \tag{2.1a}$$

$$\bar{a}_2 = a_{20} \exp[i(wt + \bar{k}.\bar{r} + \delta)], \tag{2.1b}$$

where $\delta$ is the phase difference between them. When these two waves are superposed, the total amplitude $\bar{a}$ at any point is the sum of $\bar{a}_1$ and $\bar{a}_2$ i.e.,

$$\bar{a} = \bar{a}_1 + \bar{a}_2 \tag{2.2}$$

All the known detectors say photographic emulsion, eye, photomultiplier, etc. respond to the absolute square of amplitude, i.e., irradiance at optical frequencies. The photographic emulsion responds to ($J/m^2$), while the photomultiplier to ($J$/sec.). The quantity that is detected, and which is called irradiance, $I$ is, therefore, given by

$$I = \bar{a}\,\bar{a}^* = I_1 + I_2 + 2\sqrt{I_1 I_2}\,\cos\delta \tag{2.3}$$

where $I_1$ and $I_2$ are the irradiances of the individual waves and * indicates complex conjugate of the quantity. Therefore, the resultant irradiance in the superposition region will vary with the phase difference $\delta$. It will be maximum whenever

$$\delta = 2\,m\,\pi \tag{2.4a}$$

and minimum whenever

$$\delta = (2m + 1)\,\pi\,;\quad \text{where } m = 0, \pm 1, \pm 2, \ldots \tag{2.4b}$$

is called the order of fringe.

In short, the constructive and destructive interference takes place when the waves meet in phase and anti-phase respectively. Spatial variation of irradiance is the interference pattern. Wherever the condition of constructive interference is satisfied, a bright fringe is said to have formed. Similarly, a dark fringe forms at places of destructive interference. The fringe corresponding to $m = 0$ (zero-order) is always bright. The fringe contrast or the visibility $V$ of the fringes is defined as

$$V = \frac{I_{max} - I_{min}}{I_{max} + I_{min}} = \frac{2\sqrt{I_1 I_2}}{I_1 + I_2} \rightarrow 1 \ (\text{when } I_1 = I_2) \tag{2.5}$$

$I_{max}$ and $I_{min}$ are the maximum and minimum irradiances in the resultant irradiance distribution. Obviously, the visibility of fringes is unity when the amplitudes of the interfering waves are equal. When waves are derived by amplitude division, a phase change of $\pi$ occurs at reflection. The beam reflected from the denser medium suffers a phase change of $\pi$. The conditions of constructive and destructive interference are now reversed. The zero-order fringe is dark.

The phase change of $\pi$ on reflection can be easily demonstrated by a number of experiments. The Lloyd's mirror experiment is one such simple experiment.

**Experiment 2.1:** Demonstration of phase change of $\pi$ on reflection.

**Equipments:** A gas laser, a microscope objective (40X) on an adjustable mount, a glass plate, a projection lens, white light source and a screen.

**Procedure:** The schematic of the experimental setup is shown in Fig. 2.1. A plate of ordinary glass of about 20 cm in length and 5 cm in width is positioned on a stage. One of the ends of the plate is silvered and the bottom surface is matt ground. The laser beam is focussed slightly above the top surface of the plate with a microscope objective (40X). A part of the diverging beam is reflected off the top surface of the plate. The fringe pattern on the screen is formed due to the interference between the direct going wave and the wave reflected from the upper surface of the plate. In this experiment, like in the famous Young's double slit experiment, the two waves are derived by division of wavefront. At grazing incidence the reflectivity of the surface is very high and hence both the waves, direct and reflected, are almost of equal amplitudes. The Lloyd's fringes are naturally of good contrast.

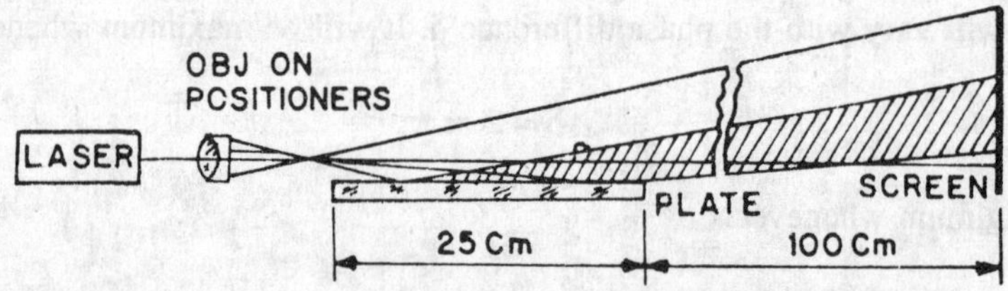


Fig. 2.1 Interference with Lloyd's Mirror

In order to observe the fringe pattern the plate is aligned (raised and tilted) on its mount such that the direct and reflected waves are superposed on the screen. Straight line fringes may then be observed. The spacing of the fringes is varied by changing the position of the focussed spot relative to the upper surface of the plate. The fringes are made to run parallel to the surface by tilting the plate. It may be noted that the fringe are not smooth but kinky due to the irregularity on the surface of the plate of an ordinary glass.

In order to demonstrate the phase change of $\pi$ on reflection, we have to look for the zero order fringe. It is obvious that the zero order fringe will be formed at the edge of the upper surface of the plate where the path difference between direct and reflected waves is zero. At a point on any other plane, the reflected wave would have travelled a longer path than the direct wave. The zero-order fringe should appear dark if a phase change of $\pi$ takes place on reflection. The zero-order fringe can be recorded by placing a photographic plate in contact with the plate and exposing it to the interference pattern. Alternatively the fringe pattern along with the edge of the plate can be imaged on a plane. This is accomplished by illuminating the edge that is silvered by white light. The edge of the plate appears brightly lit in the image. The fringe pattern obtained with this kind of arrangement is shown in Fig. 2.2. Evidently a dark fringe is formed in the immediate vicinity of the edge establishing a change of phase of $\pi$ on reflection.

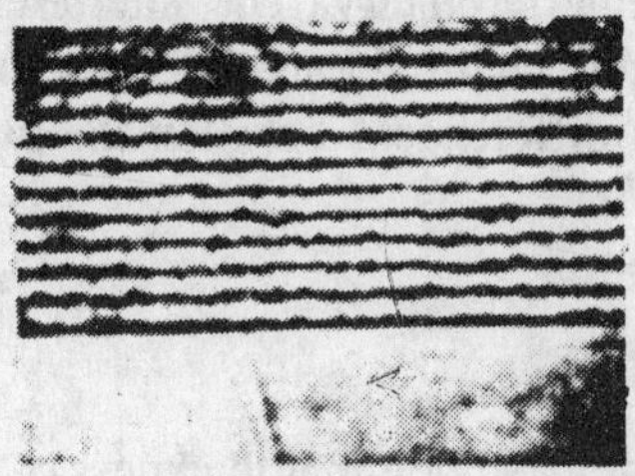


**Fig. 2.2** Interference Pattern Obtained from Lloyd's Mirror

## 2.2 Interference between Two Waves Derived by Amplitude Division

In the earlier section a simple experiment to demonstrate a phase change of $\pi$ occurring on reflection from the denser medium has been described. The two waves are derived by 'wavefront division'. We now study the interference phenomenon between two waves derived by 'amplitude division' as shown in Fig. 2.3. A ray of light is incident at an angle $\theta$ on the plate; a part of the light is reflected from the upper surface constituting a reflected ray and the remaining part is transmitted. At the bottom surface of the plate both reflection and refraction take place. In fact an incident ray is multiply reflected within the glass plate. The

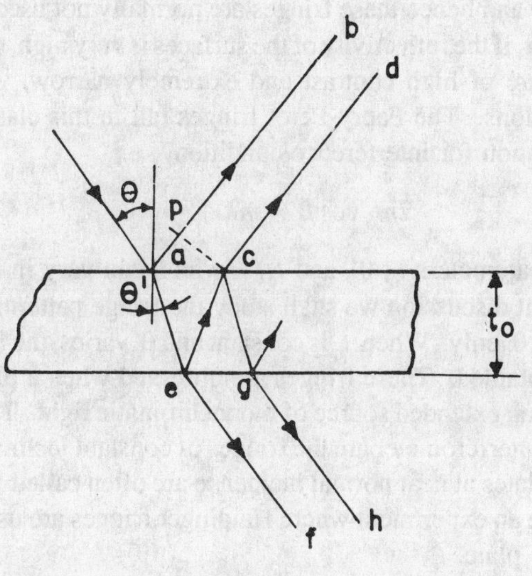


**Fig. 2.3** Interference by Amplitude Division

multiple reflections give rise to a number of reflected and transmitted rays. Let us assume that only first two rays are effectively contributing to the interference, i.e., we limit ourselves to two beam interferometry. The interference is observed between the rays *ab* and *cd* in the reflected light and between the rays *ef* and *gh* in the transmitted light. The path difference $\Delta$ between the two reflected rays is

$$\Delta = n\,(ae + ce) - ap \tag{2.6a}$$

$$= 2nt_0 \cos\theta' \tag{2.6b}$$

where $n$ and $t_0$ are the refractive index and nominal thickness of the plate, and $\theta'$ is the angle of refraction.

Since the ray *ab* suffers a phase change of $\pi$ on reflection at *a*, the complete expression for the path difference is

$$\Delta = 2nt_0 \cos\theta' - \lambda/2 \tag{2.7}$$

The conditions of constructive and destructive interference in reflected pattern are given by

$$2nt_0 \cos\theta' = (m + 1/2)\,\lambda \qquad \text{(constructive)} \tag{2.8a}$$

$$= m\lambda \qquad \text{(destructive)} \tag{2.8b}$$

For the transmitted rays, *ef* and *gh*, there is no phase change on reflection as the reflection occurs always at the rarer medium. Thus the above conditions for interference are reversed. The interference patterns in reflected and transmitted light are, therefore, complementary. The contrast of the fringes in transmitted light is extremely poor and hence these fringes are normally not used for any practical purpose. However, if the reflectivity of the surfaces is very high, the fringes formed in transmission are of high contrast and extremely narrow. These find many practical applications. The Fabry-Perot fringes fall in this class. We shall now examine the equation for interference condition, i.e.,

$$2nt_0 \cos\theta' = m\lambda \tag{2.9}$$

There are three parameters $t_0$, $\theta'$, and $t_0/\lambda$ which can vary in Eq. (2.9). For the purpose of present discussion we shall study the fringe patterns that arise due to variation in $t_0$ and $\theta'$ only. When $t_0$ is constant and $\theta'$ varies, the fringes of constant inclination are obtained. These fringes are observed when a plane parallel plate is illuminated by an extended source of monochromatic light. The fringes formed in a Fabry-Perot interferometer are the fringes of constant inclination. The fringes formed in thick plates at near normal incidence are often called Haidinger fringes. We shall describe an experiment where Haidinger fringes are used to measure the angle of a wedge plate.

When $\theta'$ is constant and $t$ varies, one obtains fringes of constant thickness. The fringes obtained when a glass plate is illuminated by a collimated beam are of constant thickness. Newton's rings are another example of fringes of constant thickness. These fringes are primarily used to test the optical components for their performance.

**Experiment 2.2:** To demonstrate the fringes of constant thickness.

**Equipments:** A gas laser, a beam expander, an ordinary glass plate and a screen.

**Procedure:** The beam from a laser oscillating in $TEM_{00}$ mode is expanded to a convenient size of 50 mm diameter with an appropriate beam expander. The collimation of the beam is checked according to the procedure described in Appendix B. The glass plate is kept in the collimated beam. It can be inclined at an angle θ with the beam, and the interference pattern is observed in reflection and transmission as shown in Fig. 2.4. The angle of incidence θ is constant over the whole plate and the fringes are loci of $2nt \cos\theta'$, where θ' is the angle of refraction in the plate and is constant.

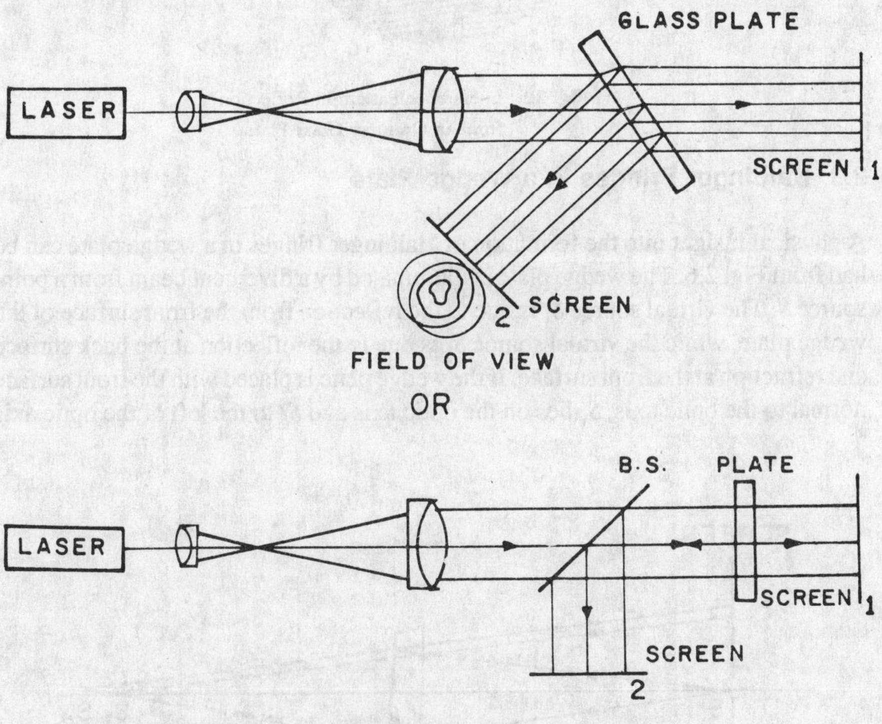


**Fig. 2.4** Interference with a Glass Plate
1. In Transmission and 2. In Reflection

Alternatively the plate is placed normal to the beam. The reflected beam retraces the beam path. The interference is observed with the help of a beam splitter that directs the reflected beams usually orthogonal to the incidence beam as shown in Fig. 2.4. The fringes are loci of $2nt$. The fringes, therefore, map the optical path. If both the thickness and refractive index of the plate are constant, the interference pattern will be of uniform illumination.

The fringes in transmission are observed by placing the screen in the transmitted beam. It may be noted that the contrast of fringes is exceedingly poor, and the fringe pattern is complementary to that observed in reflected light. Figure 2.5 shows an interferogram in reflection of an ordinary piece of plate glass.

**Fig. 2.5** Inteference Pattern in Reflection from an Ordinray Glass Plate

## 2.3 Haidinger Fringes in a Wedge Plate

A physical insight into the formation of Haidinger fringes in a wedge plate can be had from Fig. 2.6. The wedge plate is illuminated by a divergent beam from a point source $S$. The virtual source $S_1$ is due to the reflection from the front surface of the wedge plate, while the virtual source $S_2$ is due to the reflection at the back surface and refraction at the front surface. If the wedge plate is placed with the front surface normal to the optic axis, $S_1$ lies on the optic axis and $S_2$ to the left of the optic axis

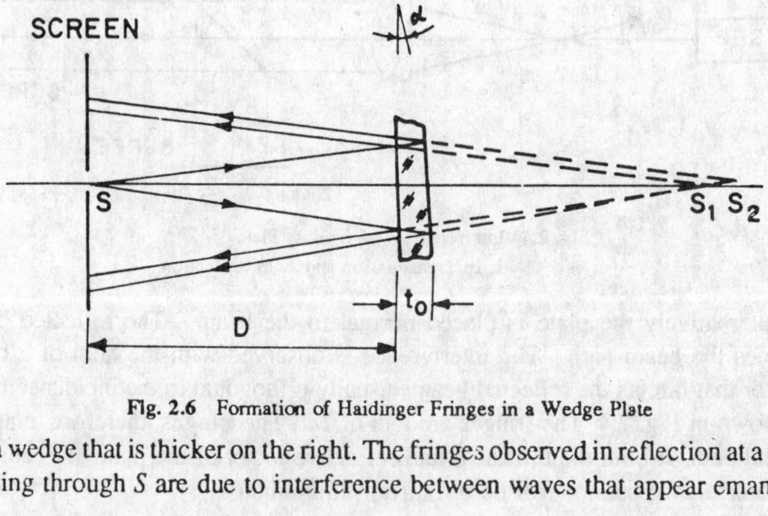


**Fig. 2.6** Formation of Haidinger Fringes in a Wedge Plate

for a wedge that is thicker on the right. The fringes observed in reflection at a plane passing through $S$ are due to interference between waves that appear emanating from $S_1$ and $S_2$ respectively. From such a qualitative virtual source picture, it may be seen that the center of the fringe pattern lies where the line joining $S_1S_2$ intersects the plane passing through $S$. Further it can be shown that the wedge angle $\alpha$, under small angle approximation, is given by*

$$\alpha = \frac{t_0 d}{2n^2D^2} \text{ (radians)} \tag{2.10}$$

where $t_0$ is the nominal thickness of the wedge plate of refractive index $n$, $d$ is the distance on the screen between the point source $S$ and the center of the fringe pattern, and $D$ is the distance between the screen and the front surface of the wedge plate. It may be noted that the fringe pattern is centered on $S$ for a plane parallel plate, and it shifts always towards the thicker end of the wedge plate.

The method provides a quick way of finding the angles of wedge plates and is particularly well suited for checking the parallelism of Brewster windows used in lasers.

**Experiment 2.3:** To measure the angle of a wedge plate using Haidinger fringes.

**Equipments:** A gas laser, a lens of a short focal length or 10X microscope objective, a screen with a pin-hole and a wedge plate on a mount.

**Procedure:** A card board or a hylem sheet having a pin-hole (~ 1 mm diameter) and with a white paper pasted on one of its sides acts as a screen. This is an essential element and is mounted normal to the unexpanded laser beam. A short focal length lens focuses the beam on to the pin-hole; the outgoing wave is thus divergent. The wedge plate whose angle is to be measured is placed in the divergent beam as shown in Fig. 2.7. The fringes due to interference between waves reflected from the front and back surfaces of the wedge are observed on the screen. If the surfaces of the plate are parallel, a pattern of circular fringes whose center is coincident with the pin-hole is observed. If there is a finite angle enclosed between the surface of the plate, the center of the fringe pattern is displaced: the shift being always towards the thicker end of the plate. The shape of the fringes is elliptical but the ellipticity is so small that the fringes could be assumed circular for all practical purposes. The shift $d$ of the center of the fringe pattern and the pin-hole can be measured fairly accurately. Also the distance between the screen and the front face of the plate can be measured accurately. The wedge angle $\alpha$ of the plate of refractive index $n$ and nominal thickness $t_0$ as measured by a micrometer screw is given by

$$\alpha = \frac{t_0 d}{2n^2D^2} \text{ (radians)} \tag{2.10}$$

$$= \frac{t_0 d}{n^2D^2} \times 10^5 \text{ (sec of an arc)}$$

*J.H. Wasilik, T.V. Blomquist, and C.S. Willet, Measurement of parallelism of the surfaces of a transparent sample using two beam non-localized fringes produced by a laser, Applied Optics, 10, 2107-12(1971).

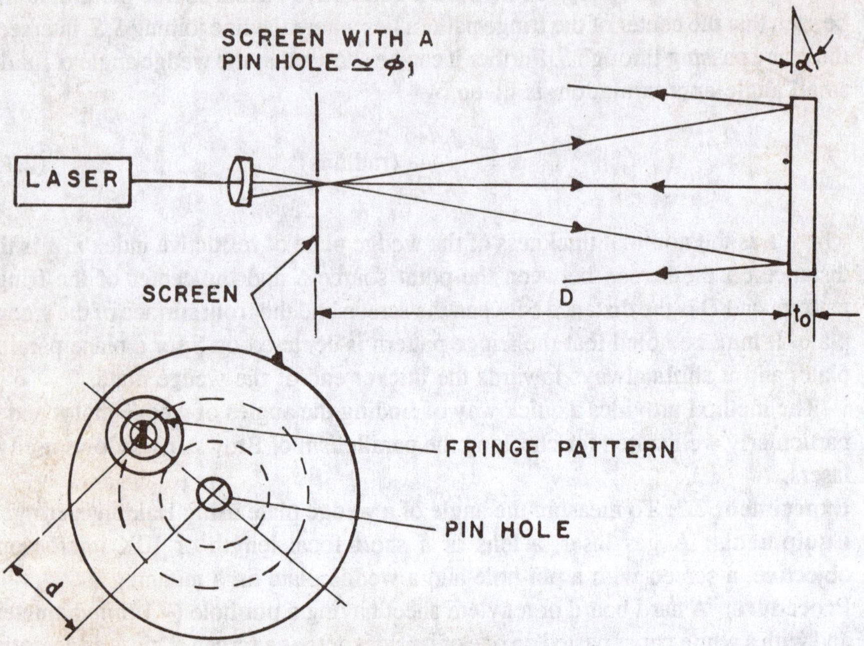


**Fig. 2.7** Determination of the Angle of a Wedge

Figure 2.8 shows photographs of the fringe pattern. In this example a glass plate of refractive index 1.51 and nominal thickness of 2 mm is placed at a distance of 260 mm from the screen. The shift of center of the fringe pattern as measured from the pin-hole is 23.5 mm. The angle of the wedge is, therefore, 26.6 sec of an arc. The experiment can be performed at a number of planes distant $D_1$, $D_2$, $D_3$, ... and corresponding shifts $d_1$, $d_2$, $d_3$... of the interference pattern may be measured. A graph between $d$ and $D^2$ may then be drawn and the value of α obtained from the slope of this line.

If the parallelism between the surfaces of the plates is to be routinely checked as may be required for the fabrication of Brewster windows for lasers, circles with

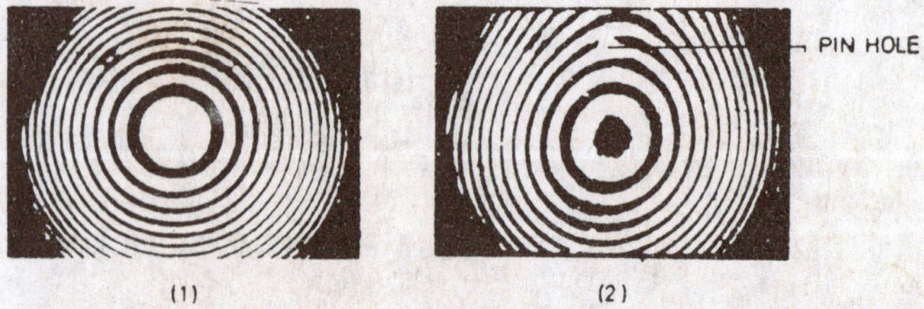


**Fig. 2.8** Fringe Pattern Obtained from: (1) Parallel Plate and (2) Wedge Plate

the pin-hole as the center for known values of angles for plates of constant nominal thickness and fixed value of $D$ may be drawn on the screen. The shift of the pattern to outside a specified circle may be taken as a criterion for the rejection of the plate.

## 2.4 Twyman-Green Interferometer

Due to long coherence length of laser light it is possible to observe interference phenomenon over the longer path differences than it was hitherto possible. Further due to its high irradiance, the interference pattern can be projected on screen. Therefore, the phenomena like diffusion reactions, evaporation processes, solution processes, heat transfer, etc. are quite easy to demonstrate. Further the use of laser as a light source has resulted in a very convenient handling and operation of the many interferometers employed for optical testing.

One of the simple interferometers which is used for optical testing and can also be used to demonstrate processes mentioned earlier is a modified Michelson interferometer and is called Twyman-Green interferometer. A schematic of the interferometer is shown in Fig. 2.9. The beam from the laser is suitably expanded and collimated using a beam-expander. The collimated beam is incident on a 50% beam splitter: the beam splitter is essentially a wedge plate in order to avoid multiply reflected beams going in the direction of main beam and consequently resulting in the spurious interference patterns due to the high irradiance and coherence of the laser light. The two beams derived at the beam splitter travel along the paths $BM_1$ and $BM_2$ and strike the mirrors $M_1$ and $M_2$ respectively. Both the mirrors are on adjustable mounts so that the reflected beams from mirrors $M_1$ and $M_2$ can be accurately manouvered and superposed for interference. The interference is observed between the beam reflected from $M_1$ and transmitted through the beam splitter, and the beam reflected from $M_2$ and also from the beam splitter. A lens $L_2$ projects the fringes on the screen. One of the mirrors say $M_2$ is mounted on an accurately made translation stage and hence can be either translated manually or by a motor. The path difference between the two interfering beams can be continuously varied.

In order to understand the working of the interferometer, one can assume that the fringe pattern arises due to interference taking place at a virtual air film enclosed between the mirror $M_1$ (say) and virtual image of the mirror $M_2$ formed in the beam splitter. If the virtual image of $M_2$ is parallel to $M_1$, the virtual air film will be of constant thickness. The two plane waves will have a constant optical path difference equal to twice the film thickness and the interference pattern will be of uniform illumination. If, however, the path difference variations occur over the field, the fringes will be formed. The fringes are loci of constant optical path. In practice one beam acts as a reference, while the other beam passes through the object and hence has path variations twice as large as in the object. The interference fringes give the shape of the object wavefront.

## 2.5 Alignment of the Interferometer

A method to obtain expanded collimated beam from the laser has been described in Appendix B. The two beams derived by the beam splitter and reflected back from the respective mirrors are to be superposed. For this purpose the mirrors are mounted on adjustable mounts. A screen is placed at the focal plane of the projection lens, where usually two bright spots will be seen. These two spots are superposed visually by adjusting the mirror mounts. After superposition the screen is moved away from the focal plane to a parallel plane where a fringe pattern is now seen. The number of fringes and their orientation can now be controlled easily by further adjusting the mirror mounts.

**Experiment 2.4:** Testing of optical components using Twyman-Green (T.G.) interferometer.

**Equipments:** A gas laser, a T.G. interferometer, optical components (a flat, a beam splitter, a prism and a lens), a camera or a screen.

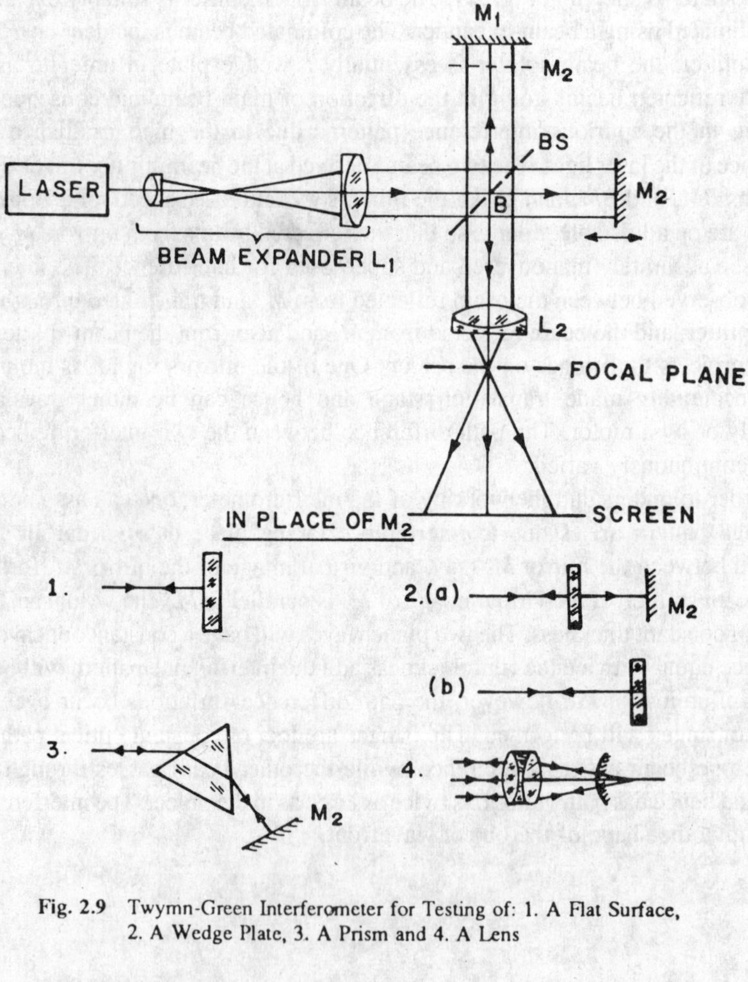


Fig. 2.9 Twymn-Green Interferometer for Testing of: 1. A Flat Surface, 2. A Wedge Plate, 3. A Prism and 4. A Lens

**Procedure:** The T.G. interferometer is used for testing the following components:

1. a surface of a component for flatness,
2. a wedge plate for the measurement of enclosed angle,
3. a prism for the shape of the wavefront, and
4. a lens for its aberrations.

For all these testing procedures, the components are such that they introduce wave front deformations of the order of a few wavelengths only. Since the reference beam is a plane wave, the aberrated wave must also be nearly plane in order to obtain a reasonable number of fringes in the field. Therefore, additional optical components may be required. The arrangement is such that an aberrated plane wave is retro-reflected. Figure 2.9 shows the arrangement for mounting the components in the interferometer.

### *1. Testing of the Surface for Flatness*

The component whose surface is to be tested for flatness replaces one of the mirrors, say $M_2$ of the interferometer. The component is so aligned as to reflect the beam back to the beam splitter where it is superposed on the beam reflected from mirror $M_1$. The interference between these two beams gives rise to the fringes which give the form of the aberrated wavefront. The interferometer is used either in the infinite or finite fringe mode. If the aberrated wavefront departs slightly from the reference wavefront, the interference pattern may hardly exhibit a fringe. The mirror is then slightly tilted, resulting in the formation of fringes. If both the wavefronts, reference and object, are collimated wavefronts, the interference pattern is well-known straight line fringe pattern. Small deformations in the object wavefront tend to introduce curvature in the fringes as shown in Fig. 2.10(1). If the fringe width and the sagitta of the fringe are $X$ and $x$ respectively, the surface is prescribed a flatness of $(x/X)\ \lambda/2$.

If the object wavefront departs considerably from the reference wavefront, but is of regular shape, circular fringes are observed in the infinite fringe setting of the interferometer. If there are $N$ circular fringes in the field of diameter $D$, the surface is prescribed a radius of curvature $R$ ($=D^2/4N\lambda$) or a flatness departure by $N\ \lambda/2$. Whether the surface is convex or concave is determined by observing the motion of fringes as the path difference is varied. For a concave surface, the fringes move inward (sink) as the path difference is decreased. Often the fringes have irregular shape, which indicates that the surface is of irregular shape.

### *2. Testing of a Wedge*

The aim is to measure the angle of the wedge enclosed between the two surfaces of the glass plate. It is assumed that the surfaces of the plate are flat and the glass medium homogeneous. There are two ways to measure the wedge-angle namely either using T.G. fringes or Fizeau fringes. When T.G. fringes are to be used, the wedge is inserted in one of the beams in the interferometer. Initially the interferometer is aligned for infinite fringe setting, i.e., the interference field is of uniform illumination. Introduction of the wedge in the beam will lead to the appearance of straight line fringes that run parallel to the apex of the wedge. If there are $N_1$ fringes in the field of diameter $D$, the angle $\alpha$ of the wedge is

$$\alpha = \frac{\lambda}{2(n-1)} \frac{N_1}{D} \tag{2.11}$$

The thicker end of the wedge can be found by locally heating the plate and observing the shift of the fringe. The fringe would always shift towards the thinner end of the plate.

When Fizeau fringes are to be used for measurement, one of the beams is completely blocked, and the wedge is kept in the other beam with the mirror removed. Indeed the T.G. interferometer is used as an arrangement to give collimated beam in which the plate is inserted. The fringe pattern arises due to the interference between the collimated beams produced by reflection from the front and back surfaces of the wedge. If there are $N_2$ fringes in the field of diameter $D$, the wedge angle $\alpha$ is

$$\alpha = \frac{\lambda}{2n} \frac{N_2}{D} \tag{2.12}$$

The Fizeau method is approximately three times more sensitive than the T.G. method for the measurement of angles of glass wedge plates. Further both the methods require the knowledge of the refractive index of the plate. However, if the measurements are made on the same plate using both the methods, the angle of the wedge can be obtained without the knowledge of the refractive index from the formula:

$$\alpha = \frac{\lambda}{2} \frac{N_2 - N_1}{D} \tag{2.13}$$

Figure 2.10(2a) gives T.G. interferogram of a wedge plate and Fig. 2.10(2b) gives Fizeau interferogram of the same plate.

### 3. *Testing of Prisms*

Both in spectroscopic and image forming instruments the prisms are used in such a way that the collimated beam incident on its entrance face emerges out as collimated beam from its exit face. On passage through the prism, the beam gets aberrated because the entrance and exit faces may not be flat and the medium may be inhomogeneous. In practice one of the prism faces is made optically flat and other face worked such that the emergent beam is collimated. This face may depart considerably from flatness but has such surface contours as to compensate for any path variations in the medium due to inhomogenieties. In T.G. interferometer we measure the departure from collimation of the beam. Depending on the type of prism examined an auxiliary arrangement is set-up in such a way that the emergent beam from the prism is reflected back through it to the beam splitter. Figure 2.9(3) shows such an arrangement for a 60° prism. The interferogram of a typical prism is shown in Fig. 2.10(3). The fringes are separated by an optical path difference of $\lambda/2$.

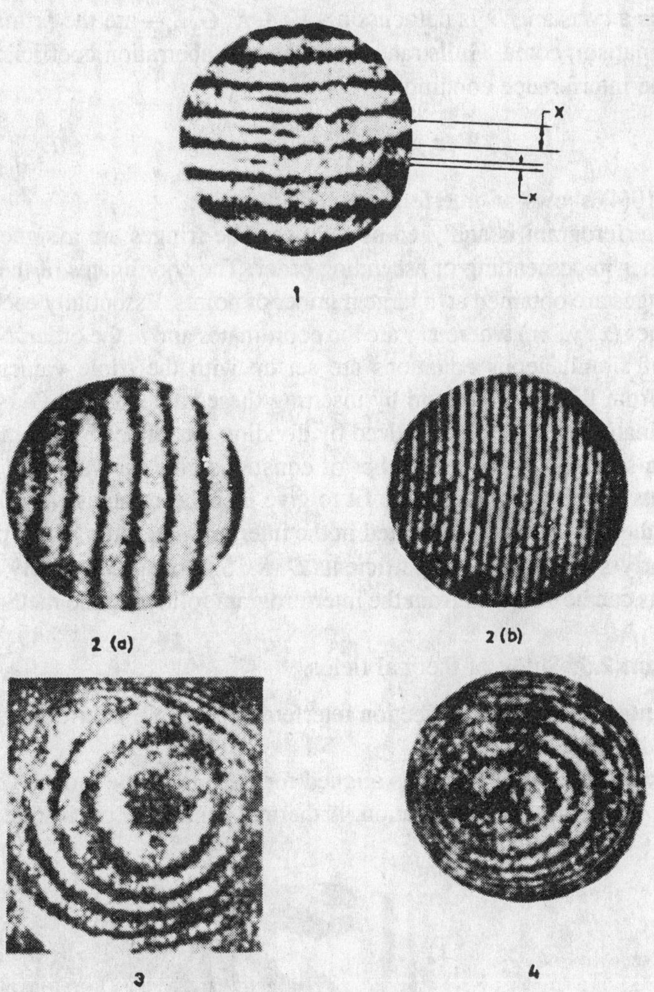


Fig. 2.10 Interferograms obtained from Twyman-Green Interferometer with: (1) A Flat Surface, [2. (a) and (b)] A Wedge Plate, (3) A Prism and (4) A Lens.

## 4. *Testing of Lens*

The lens is used with a convex mirror such that the focal point of the lens is coincident with the center of curvature of the mirror. The collimated beam through the lens is retro-reflected by the mirror and passes through it again. If the lens is well corrected, each retro-reflected ray will pass through the same zone of the lens it has earlier traversed. If the lens is moderately aberrated, a proper choice of the curvature of the mirror may nearly fulfil this requirement. The wavefront aberration function of a lens can be written as*

$$W(x,y) = C+Vx+D(x^2+y^2)+Ax^2+Kx(x^2+y^2)+S_1(x^2+y^2)^2+Gx^2(x^2+y^2)+\ldots \quad (2.14)$$

where $C$ is a constant, $D$ is defocussing, $V, A, K, G, S_1$—are the primary distortion, astigmatism, coma, Gullstrand and spherical aberration coefficients respectively. The interference condition is

$$W(x,y) = m\frac{\lambda}{2} : m \text{ is an integer} \quad (2.15)$$

Figure 2.10(4) shows an interferogram of a lens.

The interferogram is analyzed as follows: The fringes are assigned arbitrary orders either in descending or ascending order. The coordinates of the centers of bright fringes are obtained at a large number of points. Essentially each point has triple values ($x_i, y_i, m_i$) where $x, y$ are the coordinates and $m$ the order. Now a large number of simultaneous equations are set up with the triple values ($x_i, y_i, m_i$) obtained from the interferogram by inserting these values in Eq. (2.14). Usually the coordinates ($x_i, y_i$) are normalized by dividing the values by the radius of the pupil. The solutions of large number of equations give the values of aberration coefficients which are least square fit to give their best values with the errors.

When the lens is axially mounted in the interferometer, the fringe pattern will be circularly symmetric, the coefficients $D, S_1, S_2$—of the circularly symmetric aberrations can be obtained from the interferogram following the method outlined above.

**Experiment 2.5:** Study of thermal fields.

**Equipments:** A gas laser, projection interferometer (T.G. interferometer), a heat source and a screen.

**Procedure:** The interferometer is aligned for infinite fringe mode. The interference field is of constant illumination. A thermal source is now inserted in one of

**Fig. 2.11** TG Interferogram of a Candle Flame

*F.A. Sunder-Plassmann, Off axis wave aberrations and optical transfer function of an objective lens, Optik, 26, 284-8 (1967/68).

the arms of the interferometer. This would perturb the constancy of optical path difference between the interfering beams resulting in a fringe pattern characteristic of the thermal field. One can indeed calculate the changes of refractive index or the thermal gradients from the interferogram. Figure 2.11 shows a photograph of an interference pattern when a flame is inserted in one of the arms of the interferometer.

**Experiment 2.6:** To test a lens using shear interferometry.

**Equipments:** A gas laser, a microscope objective and a pin-hole on a mount, lens on a mount for testing, a plane parallel plate (shear plate) on a rotatable mount and a screen.

**Procedure:** The shear interferometery is used to evaluate the performance of a lens when used on axis. Therefore, only defocussing and spherical aberration of a lens can be measured. It is, therefore, recommended for evaluating achromates.

Figure 2.12 (a) shows the experimental arrangement. The laser beam is expanded and filtered by a microscope objective and a pin-hole assembly. The lens is positioned in the divergent beam such that its focal point is close to the pin-hole. The beam transmitted through the lens is near collimated. The plane parallel plate (ppp) is kept at an angle in the beam and the interference pattern is observed on a screen in the reflected beams.

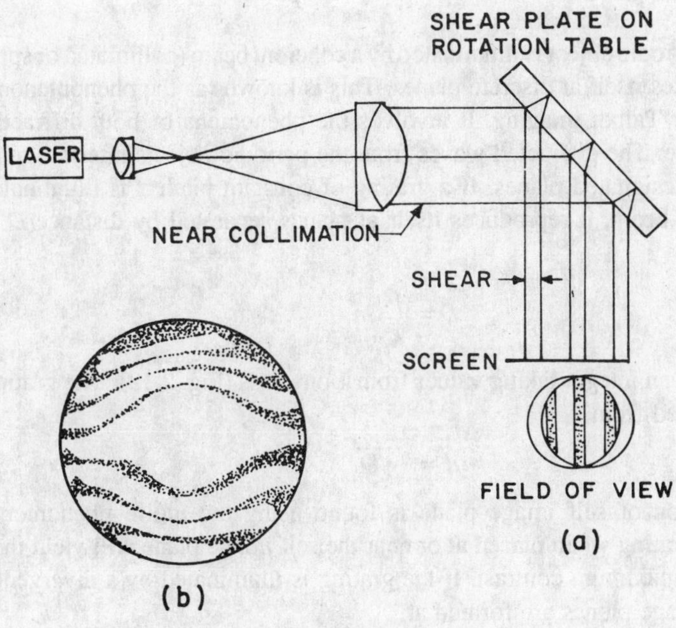


**Fig. 2.12** (a) Plane Parallel Plate Shearing Interferometer
(b) Shear Interferogram of a Lens

If the test lens is free from spherical aberration, straight line fringes will be observed whose number decreases when the test lens is translated axially such that its focal point approaches the pin-hole. When the focal point is coincident with the pin-hole, the field appears uniformly illuminated. This procedure is adopted for obtaining a collimated beam. In the presence of spherical aberration the fringe pattern would have curved fringes. The defocusing is so adjusted that there are 5 to 6 fringes in the field, and the interference pattern is then photographed. A typical interferogram of a lens is shown in Fig. 2.12 (b).

The wavefront aberration function of a lens when used on axis is given by

$$W(x, y) = C + D\,(x^2+y^2) + S_1\,(x^2+y^2)^2 + \ldots \tag{2.16}$$

where $C$ is a constant, $D$ is defocussing parameter and $S_1$ is the primary spherical aberration coefficient. The shear interferometry senses the gradient of $W(x, y)$. The fringes are formed whenever

$$2Dx\Delta x + 4S_1\, x\Delta x\,(x^2+y^2) = m\lambda \tag{2.17}$$

where $\Delta x$ is the shear along $x$—direction and is assumed very small.

The interferogram is evaluated at grid points or along the fringes giving a number of triple values $(x_i, y_i, m_i)$. An arbitrary fringe order is assigned to any fringe, and other fringes are labelled with respect to this fringe order. A number of simultaneous equations are set up for these triple values. The solution of these equations gives the values of $D$ and $S_1$, which are later best fit to give the best values along with the errors.

## 2.6 Self Imaging

When a periodic object is illuminated by a coherent beam (collimated or spherical), it reproduces itself at discrete planes. This is known as the phenomenon of self imaging or Talbot imaging. It involves the phenomena of both diffraction and interference. The diffracted waves from the periodic objects interfere to give an image at designated planes. If a grating of constant pitch $d$ is illuminated by a collimated beam, it reproduces itself at planes separated by distance $D$ from it where

$$D = \frac{d^2}{\lambda}\, m \tag{2.18}$$

where $m$ is an integer taking values from 1 onwards (Fig. 2.13). The grating pitch $d$ is obtained from

$$d = \sqrt{\lambda D} \tag{2.19}$$

The location of self image plane is found using the moire phenomenon. An identical grating when placed at or near the self image plane will yield the moire fringes of maximum contrast. If the grating is illuminated by a divergent beam, the self image planes are formed at

$$z = \frac{mD}{1 - mD/R} \tag{2.20}$$

where $D$ is the self image distance in the collimated beam and $R$ is the distance between the grating and the point source. The grating pitch at the first self image plane is

$$d_s = d\left[\frac{R+z}{R}\right] \tag{2.21}$$

The grating pitch increased as if it is projected.

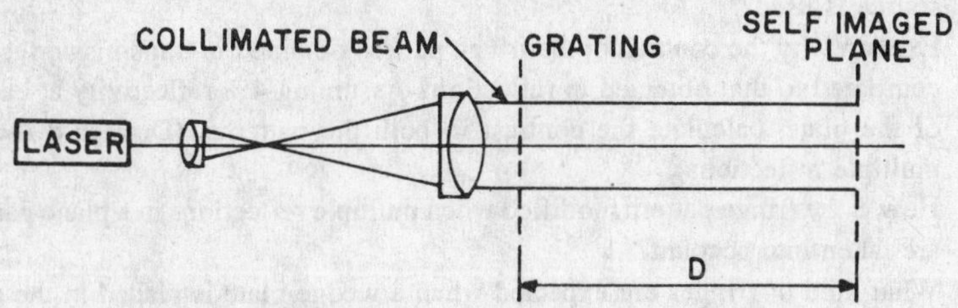


**Fig. 2.13** Self Imaging-Measurement of Grating Pitch

**Experiment 2.7:** To determine the grating pitch using the phenomenon of self imaging.

**Equipments:** A gas laser, a beam expander, a pair of identical gratings, a screen.

**Procedure:** The laser beam is expanded and collimated to a size of about 25 mm in diameter. A coarse grating (2*l*/mm) is placed in the collimated beam. The grating will be imaged at a number of planes. The distances between the grating plane and successive image planes are measured with a meter scale, and an average value of $D$ is obtained.

If another grating of the same pitch is available, it can be used to locate self imaged planes by observing the moire 'fringes between them. At the self imaged plane, the moire' pattern is sharp; on either side of this diffuse moire' fringes of decreasing contrast are observed.

The value of the grating pitch $d$ is obtained from the relation

$$d = \sqrt{D\lambda}$$

An accuracy of 1% in the measurement of $D$ leads to an accuracy of 0.5% in the calculated value of $d$.

It is possible to use this phenomenon to study the disturbance caused by thermal, pressure fields, etc. The second grating is so adjusted that it is shifted by half the period with respect to the self image of the first grating resulting in the dark field. Any disturbance would result in the appearance of light distribution in the field. The accuracy of the method increases when higher order self image planes are used.

## PROBLEMS

1. What happens to the interference pattern when a front coated mirror is used instead of a glass plate in Lloyd's mirror experiment?
2. Suggest some other arrangements for observing interference of light using wavefront division. Elaborate on the nature of fringe pattern in each case.
3. In Lloyd's mirror experiment, the virtual image is inverted with respect to the real image. What effect does it have on the appearance of fringes when an extended slit source is used?
4. Explain why the contrast in the fringe pattern obtained in transmission is very poor compared to that obtained in reflection? Assuming 4% reflectivity at each surface of the plate, calculate the contrast in both the patterns. (Disregard the effect of multiple reflections).
5. How is the fringe pattern modified when multiple reflections in a plane parallel plate are taken into account?
6. What kind of fringes are expected when a wedge plate is placed in the collimated beam? Can we obtain the wavelength of light by measuring the fringe width and the angle of the wedge and to what accuracy?
7. How is the fringe pattern of a wedge having high reflectivity surfaces is modified?
8. Compare the Haidinger fringe, T.G. fringe and Fizeau fringe methods for measuring the angle of a wedge.
9. Set up an auxiliary optical arrangement for testing a constant deviation prism.
10. Adopt T.G. interferometer for the measurement of length. State its drawbacks and suggest a suitable configuration for the length interferometer.
11. A convenient method to test the surfaces is to observe fringes in an air film enclosed between the master surface and the test surface. The arrangement is illuminated by a broad source. The fringes thus obtained are the fringes of constant thickness. Comment.

# 3. Diffraction of Light

The phenomena of interference and diffraction are the manifestations of the wave nature of light. Diffraction is very often referred to as the bending of the waves round an obstacle. However, whenever wave is limited in spatial extent by an aperture or an obstacle, diffraction takes place.

The phenomenon of diffraction is studied under two heads, namely Fresnel and Fraunhofer diffraction theories. Fraunhofer diffraction is a special case of Fresnel diffraction when the source illuminatiing the aperture and the observation screen are located at infinity. When an aperture is illuminated by a collimated beam, and the diffraction pattern is observed at infinity, we are studying the Fraunhofer diffraction pattern of the aperture. Often a lens is inserted after the aperture, and the diffraction pattern is studied at its back focal plane.

The study of Fresnel diffraction is of academic interest only. On the other hand, Fraunhofer diffraction plays an important role both in the imaging and spectroscopic instruments. The resolving power of a telescope, a microscope or any other imaging instrument is governed by Fraunhofer diffraction. Fortunately, it is very easy to handle it mathematically. Following Huygen's-Fresnel diffraction theory, the amplitude distribution at any point $P$ in the Fraunhofer region of an aperture is given by

$$u(p,q) = c \iint_{-\infty}^{\infty} t(x,y)\, e^{ik(px+qy)}\, dx dy \qquad (3.1)$$

where $t(x, y) = 1$ inside the aperture

$= 0$ otherwise,

$p$ and $q$ are the direction cosines of point $P$, and $c$ is complex constant. If the pattern is observed at the back focal plane of a lens, then $p=x'/f$ and $q=y'/f$ where $(x', y')$ are the cartesian coordinates of the point $P$. This equation also describes a Fourier transform relationship between $u(p, q)$ and $t(x, y)$.

In what follows we shall examine the Fraunhofer diffraction patterns of some simple apertures and study their practical utility. The Fraunhofer diffraction pattern has been utilized for the measurement of shapes and sizes of the apertures. The size of a hole and its circularity can be esaily measured from the study of its diffraction pattern.

**Fraunhofer Diffraction at a Slit**

We consider a slit of width $2b$ that is infinitely long along $y$ direction. It is illuminated by a collimated beam as shown in Fig. 3.1. The slit is mathematically defined as

$$t(x) = 1 : -b < x < b \\ = 0 \text{ ; otherwise} \tag{3.2}$$

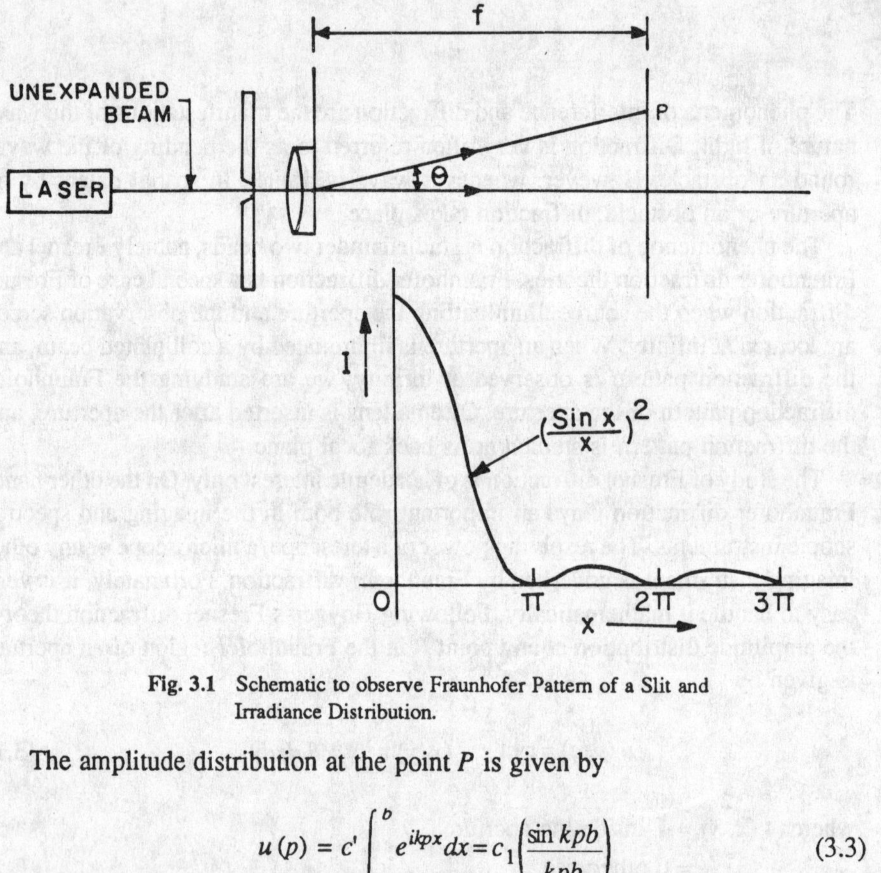


**Fig. 3.1** Schematic to observe Fraunhofer Pattern of a Slit and Irradiance Distribution.

The amplitude distribution at the point $P$ is given by

$$u(p) = c' \int_{-b}^{b} e^{ikpx} dx = c_1 \left(\frac{\sin kpb}{kpb}\right) \tag{3.3}$$

where $c'$ and $c_1$ are complex constants.

The irradiance distribution is expressed as

$$I(p) = I_0 \left(\frac{\sin kpb}{kpb}\right)^2 \tag{3.4}$$

where $I_0$ is the irradiance at $p = 0$. The irradiance distribution $I(p)$ as a function of $kpb$ is shown in Fig. 3.1. The minima of irradiance distribution occur when

$$k\, pb = m\pi$$

or

$$\frac{x'_m}{f} = \frac{m\lambda}{2b} \tag{3.5}$$

where $x'_m$ is the value of $x'$ corresponding to the $m$th minimum. We can also write $\sin \theta_m = x'_m/f$, and hence the diffraction angle $\theta_m$ for the $m$th minimum is given by

$$\sin \theta_m = \frac{m\lambda}{2b} \tag{3.6}$$

The condition $m = 0$ gives the maximum irradiance $I_0$ that occurs in the direction $\theta_m = 0$. The angular separation between the consecutive minima is $\lambda/2b$: the only exception being the first order minima about the central maximum which are $\lambda/b$ apart. It can also be shown that secondary maxima are also $\lambda/2b$ apart. The central maximum, therefore, has twice the width of the secondary maxima.

It may be seen that the secondary maxima come closer as the slit width $2b$ is increased. In the extreme case when $2b = \infty$, no diffraction takes place. Indeed a diffraction strain gauge can be set up by mounting the jaws of the slit on a member which is subjected to the load. Figure 3.2 (a), (b) and (c) shows diffraction patterns of slits of different widths.

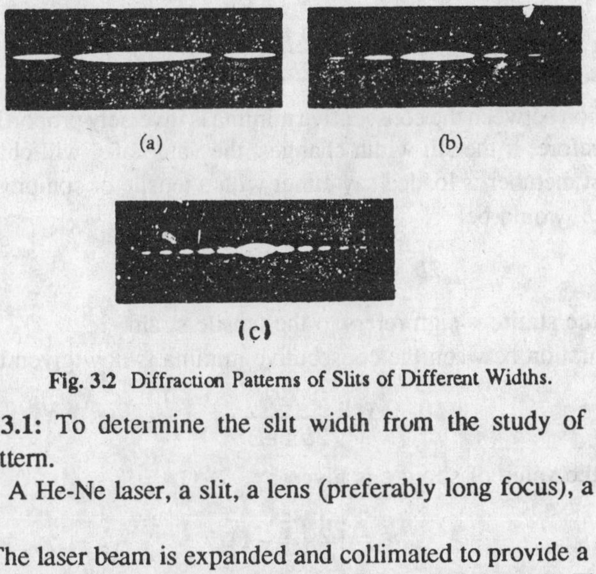

Fig. 3.2 Diffraction Patterns of Slits of Different Widths.

**Experiment 3.1:** To determine the slit width from the study of Fraunhofer diffraction pattern.

**Equipments:** A He-Ne laser, a slit, a lens (preferably long focus), a screen and a scale.

**Procedure:** The laser beam is expanded and collimated to provide a beam of 15 to 20 mm in diameter. The schematic of the set up is shown in Fig. 3.1. The diffraction pattern is observed at the focal plane of the lens. In practice the slit is kept close to the lens but its location is immaterial. On the screen located at the focal plane, the positions of minima of irradiance distribution are marked. The positions of the minima are measured by a millimeter scale if a long focal length (>1 m) lens is used.

A graph between the positions of minima and the order can be drawn using the method of least squares.

From the fomula, the slit width is given by

$$2b = f\lambda \frac{m - m'}{x_m - x_{m'}} \tag{3.7a}$$

The quantity $(m-m')/(x_m-x'_m)$ is obtained from the graph and used for calculating the slit width.

Alternatively, the wavelength of laser light can be measured if the slit width is accurately known.

## 3.1 Diffraction Strain Gauge

A slit with independent jaws is cemented to the test member such that its jaws are parallel. The distance between the fixed points on each jaw of the slit on the test member is the gauge length. Let it be denoted by $L$.

When the Fraunhofer diffraction pattern of the slit is observed, the positions of irradiance minima are given by

$$x'_m = m\frac{\lambda f}{2b} : m = 0, \pm 1, \pm 2, \ldots \tag{3.7b}$$

The separation between the two consecutive minima is given by

$$\bar{x} = \frac{\lambda f}{2b} \tag{3.8}$$

The separation between the consecutive minima is inversely proportional to the slit width. Therefore, if the slit width changes, the value of $\bar{x}$ will change.

If the test member is loaded say either with a tensile or compressive load, the slit width $2b'$ would be

$$2b' = 2b \pm \varepsilon L \tag{3.9}$$

where $\varepsilon$ is the strain; + sign refers to the tensile strain.

The separation between the consecutive minima is now given by

$$\bar{x}' = \frac{\lambda f}{2b \pm \varepsilon L} \tag{3.10}$$

Therefore, the value of strain $\varepsilon$ is given by

$$\varepsilon = \frac{2b}{L}\left(\frac{\bar{x}}{\bar{x}'} - 1\right) \tag{3.11}$$

In practice one measures $\bar{x}$ and $\bar{x}'$ and $(2b/L)$ is taken as a parameter of the gauge.

**Experiment 3.2:** To measure the strain $\varepsilon$ with a diffraction strain gauge.

**Equipments:** A He-Ne laser, a slit with independent jaws, a model, a long focal length lens and a screen.

**Procedure:** Figure 3.3 shows an experimental set up. The model can be a bar that can be subjected to either tensile or compressive loading. The jaws of the slit are fixed to the model, and aligned such that they run parallel to each other. The beam from the laser impinges on the slit and the diffracted beam is collected by a long focus lens. The observation screen is located at the focal plane.

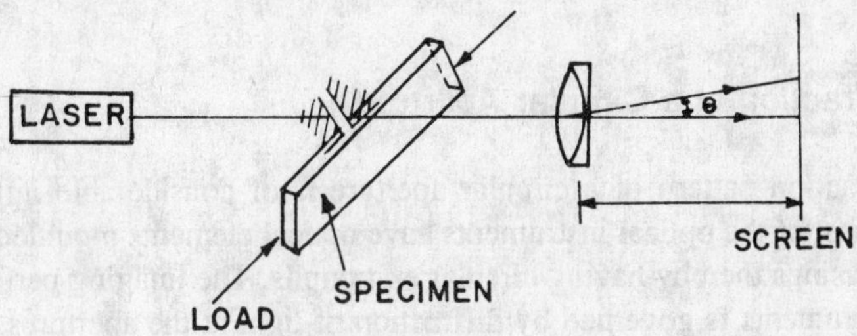


**Fig. 3.3** Diffraction Strain Gauge.

The separation $\bar{x}$ is measured at the screen for a number of minima positions and an average value of $\bar{x}$ is obtained. The model is now loaded, and the new value of separation $\bar{x}'$ is obtained by making a number of measurements. The strain is then calculated from

$$\varepsilon = \frac{2b}{L}\left(\frac{\bar{x}}{\bar{x}'} - 1\right) \tag{3.12}$$

Indeed a graph between ε and load can be plotted to verify Hooke's law.

## 3.2 Diffraction at a Wire

The diffraction pattern of a wire can be obtained from that of a slit with the help of Babinet's priniciple. If $u_1$ is the amplitude at any point on the screen due to an aperture, and $u_2$ is the amplitude at the same point due to a complementary aperture, then

$$\bar{u}_1 + \bar{u}_2 = \bar{u}_0 \tag{3.12}$$

where $\bar{u}_0$ is the amplitude at the point due to unapertured wave and hence it is constant. The amplitude $u_0$ will be confined at the optical axis of a lens and hence will be zero at any other point on a transverse plane where $\bar{u}_1 = -\bar{u}_2$. The irradiance distributions, away from the axis, will be identical for complementary apertures. A strip of width $2b$ will be a complementary aperture to a slit of width $2b$. In practice, however, we take a wire of diameter $2b$ as the complementary screen. The diameter $2b$ is, therefore, obtained as

$$2b = \lambda f \frac{m - m'}{x_m - x_{m'}} \tag{3.13}$$

where $x_m$ and $x_m'$ are the positions of *m*th and *m'*th minima respectively.

**Experiment 3.3:** To determine the thickness of sleeve on a fine wire.

**Equipments:** A He-Ne laser, a wire, a long focus lens, and a screen.

**Procedure:** The procedure for measuring the diameter of the wire is the same as that of the slit. In the first part, the diameter $2b'$ of the sleeved wire is obtained, and in the second part, the diameter $2b$ of the wire is obtained. The sleeve thickness is $(b' - b)$.

## 3.3 Diffraction at a Circular Aperture

The diffraction pattern of a circular aperture is of considerable importance in optics. Most of the optical instruments have optical elements mounted in circular shape housings thereby having circular exit pupils. The imaging performance of these instruments is governed by diffraction of light at the apertures.

The amplitude distribution $u(p, q)$ in the Fraunhofer diffraction pattern of a circular aperture of radius $R$ is given by

$$u(p,q) = c \iint_{-\infty}^{\infty} \text{circ}\left(\frac{\sqrt{x^2+y^2}}{R}\right) e^{ik(px+qy)}\, dx\, dy \tag{3.14}$$

where $\text{circ}\left(\frac{\sqrt{x^2+y^2}}{R}\right) = 1$ : in the aperture

$= 0$ : outside the aperture

Writing $x = r\cos\theta$, $y = r\sin\theta$

and $p = w\cos\phi$, $q = w\sin\phi$ the above integral is rewritten as

$$u(w,\phi) = c\int_0^{2\pi}\int_0^R e^{ikwr\cos(\theta-\phi)}\, r\, dr\, d\theta \tag{3.15}$$

This integral can be easily evaluated. Therefore,

$$u(w,\phi) = u(w) = u_0\left[\frac{2J_1(kRw)}{kRw}\right] \tag{3.16}$$

Here $w(=p/f)$ is the sine of the angle which the line from the center of the aperture to any point on the observation plane makes with the optic axis, $\rho$ is the linear distance of the point from the axis, $u_0$ is the amplitude at $w=0$, and $J_1(x)$ is the Bessel function of first order and first kind. The irradiance distribution $I(w)$ $(= uu^*)$ is called the Airy distribution.

The distribution shows a bright maximum surrounded by a number of secondary maxima of decreasing irradiances. The width of the central maximum is approximately double that of the secondary maxima. The minima occur at the zero's of the Bessel function $J_1(x)$. The first minimum occurs when

$$kRw = 3.83$$

or

$$w = \frac{1.22\lambda}{2R} \tag{3.17}$$

The angular width ($2w$) is inversely proportional to the diameter of the aperture ($2R$); smaller is the aperture, broader is the central maximum. Thus for larger apertures, the diffraction pattern is not visible to the naked eye. The experiment will, therefore, be conducted with very small apertures (pin-holes) of size about 0.1 mm in diameter.

In optical instruments like telescope, the objective itself acts as a limiting aperture, and the diffraction takes place at the rim of the lens. Assuming the objective to be aberration free, it is seen that the image of a point source at infinity will not be a point but an Airy's disc surrounded by a number of rings. The diameter ($2\rho_0$) of the Airy's disc will be

$$2\rho_0 = \frac{2.44\,\lambda f}{2R} \tag{3.18}$$

The equation suggests a method to measure the diameters of small apertures by measuring the Airy's disc diameters in the corresponding diffraction patterns. The diameter $D$ is given by

$$D = \frac{1.22\,\lambda f}{\rho_0} \tag{3.19}$$

$\rho_0$ can be measured to a fairly good accuracy. Further from the inspection of the diffraction pattern, we can conclude if the aperture is circular. A round aperture gives rise to circular symmetric fringe pattern.

**Experiment 3.4:** To study the Fraunhofer diffraction pattern of a circular aperture and to measure its diameter.

**Equipments:** A He-Ne laser, a circular aperture (a pin-hole of 0.1-0.2 mm diameter), a long focus lens, a power meter and a screen.

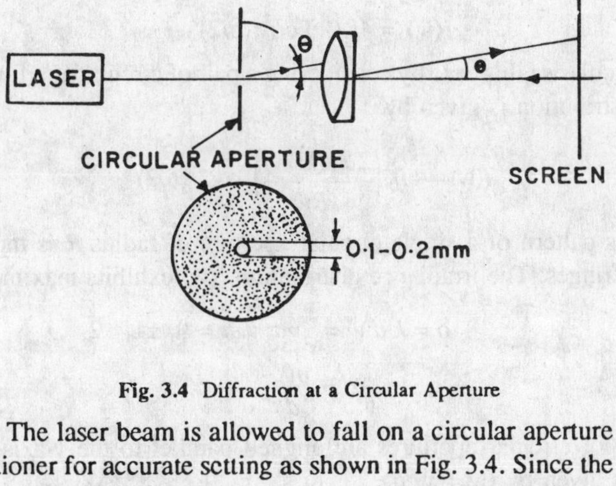


Fig. 3.4 Diffraction at a Circular Aperture

**Procedure:** The laser beam is allowed to fall on a circular aperture mounted on a $x-y$ positioner for accurate setting as shown in Fig. 3.4. Since the unexpanded beam is around 2 mm in diameter, and the aperture is 0.1 to 0.2 mm in diameter, it may be safely assumed that the aperture is illuminated by a uniform collimated wave. The diffracted field is collected by a long focus lens and the observations are made at its focal plane. The diffraction pattern of a circular hole is shown in Fig. 3.5. Only one ring is shown in the photograph.

**Fig. 3.5** Diffraction Pattern at a Circular Aperture

If the pattern is scanned along its diametrical line using a pin-hole on the power meter head, the power vs position curve can be obtained. This would resemble $\left(\frac{2J_1(x)}{x}\right)^2$ distribution.

The width of the central miximum can be obtained from this plot. This is used to calculate the diameter of the aperture. Alternatively, the width of central maximum can be obtained by marking the positions of first minima on the screen and measuring the distance between the markings. An accuracy of 0.5 mm may be sufficient in a well planned experiment.

## 3.4 Diffraction at Two Apertures

Consider two identical apertures with an inter-distance of $d$. The apertures are illuminated with a collimated beam and the amplitude distribution is studied at the focal plane of a lens. Let the amplitude at any point at the Fraunhofer plane due to diffraction at an aperture be $u_1(w)$. The amplitude at the same point due to diffraction at the other aperture will also be $u_1(w)$ but shifted by a relative phase of $\delta$. Thus the total amplitude at the point is

$$\begin{aligned} u(w) &= u_1(w) + u_1(w)\, e^{i\delta} \\ &= u_1(w)\,(1 + e^{i\delta}) \end{aligned} \tag{3.20}$$

The phase difference $\delta$ is $kdw$.

The irradiance distribution is given by

$$I(w) = 4I_1(w)\cos^2(\delta/2) \tag{3.21}$$

If we particularise this case by considering a pair of circular apertures, then the irradiance distribution is given by

$$I(w) = 4\, i_0 \left(\frac{2J_1(kRw)}{kRw}\right)^2 \cos^2(\delta/2) \tag{3.22}$$

The Airy's pattern of a single circular aperture of radius $R$ is modulated by interference fringes. The irradiance distribution $I(w)$ exhibits maxima whenever

$$\delta = k\,d\,w = 2m\pi : m = 0, \pm1, \pm2, \ldots$$

or

$$w = \frac{m\lambda}{d} \tag{3.23}$$

If the pair of circular apertures are aligned parallel to the $y$-axis, the fringe position $y_m$ is given by ($w = y_m/f$)

$$y_m = m \frac{\lambda f}{d} \tag{3.24}$$

This fringe width is

$$\bar{y} = \frac{\lambda f}{d} \tag{3.25}$$

The fringes run parallel to $x$-axis, i.e., always normal to the line joining the centers of the apertures which is parallel to $y$-axis in this particular case.

The diffraction pattern of an aperture is modulated by straight line fringes whose width is inversely proportional to the intercenter separation $d$, and whose orientation is always perpendicular to the line joining the centers. Therefore, the orientation and width of the fringes can be used to determine the separation $d$, and the orientation of apertures. Also the diameter of the circular aperture can be obtained from the study of the diffraction pattern as explained earlier.

**Experiment 3.5:** To study the Fraunhofer diffraction pattern at a pair of circular apertures, and to measure their separation.

**Equipments :** A He-Ne laser, a diaphragm containing a pair of circular apertures, a long focus lens and a screen.

**Procedure:** For convenience the pair of apertures consists of two holes of about 0.2 mm diameter, separated approx. by 0.4 mm. The diaphragm is mounted on a $x$-$y$ positioner and placed in an unexpanded laser beam. The diffracted beam is collected by a long focus lens kept very close to the diaphragm. At the focal plane, a diffraction pattern similar to that shown in Fig. 3.6 is observed. The fringe spacing can be easily measured by marking the minima positions on a graph paper that is fixed to the screen. The orientation of the pin-holes, with reference to Fig. 3.6 is horizontal.

If a diaphragm containing circular holes of larger diameters, and correspondingly larger separation is used, the laser beam is to be expanded and collimated,

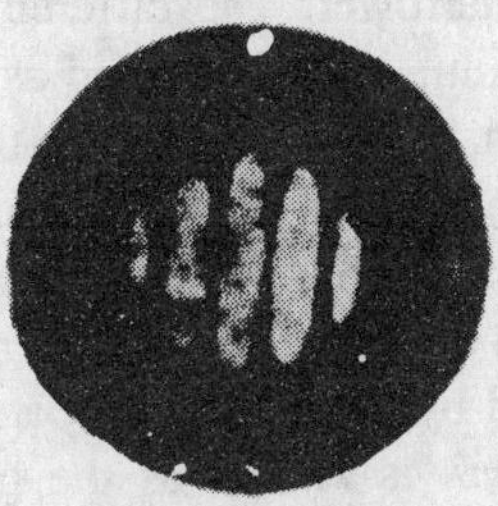

**Fig. 3.6** Diffraction Pattern of a Pair of Circular Apertures

and the fringe width is to be measured very carefully due to the contraction of the pattern. The pattern may be magnified for easy measurement but it requires the knowledge of the magnification for calculating $d$.

## 3.5 Diffraction at Multi-Apertures

Let us consider one dimensional array of $N$ apertures with the intercenter distance of $d$. The amplitude distribution at any point $P$ on the Fraunhofer plane is obtained by summing up the amplitudes due to each aperture with their proper phases. It is given by

$$u(p) = u_1(p)\,[1 + e^{i\delta} + e^{2i\delta} + \ldots + e^{i(N-1)\delta}] \qquad (3.26)$$

where $u_1(p)$ is the amplitude due to an aperture at the point $P$, and $\delta$ is the phase difference. The phase difference $\delta$ is given by $\delta = kd \sin\theta$. The irradiance distribution is given by

$$I(p) = I_1(p) \frac{\sin^2(N\delta/2)}{\sin^2(\delta/2)} \qquad (3.27)$$

where $I_1(p)$ is the irradiance distribution due to a single aperture.

If the aperture is a slit of width $2b$, the multiple aperture arrangement is known as a grating of rectangular transmission profile. The irradiance distribution at the focal plane of a lens due to diffraction at the grating is

$$I(p) = I_0 \left(\frac{\sin kpb}{kpb}\right)^2 \left(\frac{\sin N\delta/2}{\sin(\delta/2)}\right)^2 \qquad (3.28)$$

where $I_0$ is the irradiance in the direction $\theta = 0$. The term $\left(\frac{\sin N\delta/2}{\sin \delta/2}\right)^2$ represents the interference term due to $N$ slits. This modulates the diffraction pattern of a single slit. The fringes produced by interference due to $N$ slits are narrower compared to single slit diffraction pattern and hence a number of them lie in central maximum. Their locations can be determined from the consideration of interference term alone. This term gives maxima of magnitude of $N^2$ for $\delta/2 = 0, \pi, 2\pi$. These principal maxima correspond to

$$d \sin\theta = m\lambda: \quad m = 0, \pm 1, \pm 2, \ldots \qquad (3.29)$$

i.e., they appear exactly at positions corresponding to fringes in double slit interference but are very much narrower. The different integral values of $m$ give different orders of the spectrum; $m = 1$ is termed as the first order, $m = 2$ as the second order and so on. It can, however, be shown that there are $(N—1)$ minima and $(N—2)$ secondary maxima between any two consecutive principal maxima. As the number of slits $N$ increases, the magnitude of the principal maxima increases and that of the secondary maxima decreases. The irradiance distribution in any principal maxima is governed by the diffraction pattern of a single slit.

The equation $d \sin\theta = m\lambda$ is known as the grating equation for normal illumination. In general, when the beam is incident at the grating at an angle $i$, the grating equation is written as

$$d(\sin i + \sin\theta) = m\lambda. \qquad (3.30)$$

For normal incidence on grating, the measurement of angle of diffraction $\theta$ alone can be used to determine $\lambda$ when grating constant $d$ is known. If a lens of focal length $f$ is used to collect the diffracted beams, the diffraction pattern which consists of dots normal to the grating elements is obtained at its focal plane. Let the $m$th order occur at a distance $x_m$ from the optical axis, then

$$x_m = \frac{f}{d} m\lambda, \text{ provided of } x_m < f. \tag{3.31}$$

The measurement of $x_m$ is used to calculate $\lambda$ from the above equation.

**Experiment 3.6:** To determine the wavelength of laser light with a transmission grating.

**Equipments:** A He-Ne laser, a transmission grating, a long focal length lens, and a screen.

**Procedure:** The beam from a laser oscillating in $TEM_{00}$ mode is expanded and collimated to fill the grating surface. A lens of relatively large focal length $f$ is placed behind the grating to collect the diffracted beams. The spectrum in the form of dots is displayed on the screen placed at the focal plane of the lens as shown in Fig. 3.7. You may notice the decrease in the irradiance as you move away from the zeroth order towards the higher orders, i.e., the first order is brighter than the second and so on. Let $x_m$ be the distance of $m$th order from the zeroth order. The wavelength of the laser light is obtained from the relation

$$\lambda = \frac{d}{m} \sin\theta_m = \frac{d}{m} \cdot \frac{x_m}{\left(x_m^2 + f^2\right)^{1/2}}$$

**Fig. 3.7** Diffraction Pattern of a Grating

The wavelength $\lambda$ is obtained by averaging the result for many orders.

It is also possible to conduct this experiment with the unexpanded laser beam. The beam is allowed to fall over the grating and the spectrum is received on a screen sufficiently far away. The wavelength is calculated from the above equation with $f=D$, where $D$ is the distance between the plane of the grating and that of the screen. The accuracy of measurements is not very good as the various orders of the spectrum are diffuse.

It would be advisable to use this experiment to measure the grating constant of a grating as the wavelength of the laser light is pretty accurately known.

**Fig. 3.8** Diffraction Pattern of a Mesh

Instead of a grating, if a wire mesh is used for observation of the diffraction pattern, a visually impressive pattern is observed as shown in Fig. 3.8. The periodicities along $x$ and $y$ directions can be obtained from the experiment. Further any fault in the periodic structure will also be revealed as anomalies in the diffraction pattern.

**Experiment 3.7:** To measure the wavelength of He-Ne laser light with a vernier caliper.

**Equipments :** A He-Ne laser, a vernier caliper, a meter scale, millimeter graph paper, etc.

**Procedure:** This experiment was first demonstrated by Schawlow [Amer. J. Phys. 33, 922 (1965)] using a ruler. This is done here using the main scale of the vernier caliper. The scale must be engraved. The venier caliper is placed on a horizontal table, and the laser is aligned such that the unexpanded beam is incident at the grazing angle ($i$=87.0°) as shown in Fig. 3.9(a). The diffraction pattern is observed at a distance of 3 to 4 meters from the scale. The beam can be aligned so that the diffraction pattern is at its best as shown in Fig. 3.9(b).

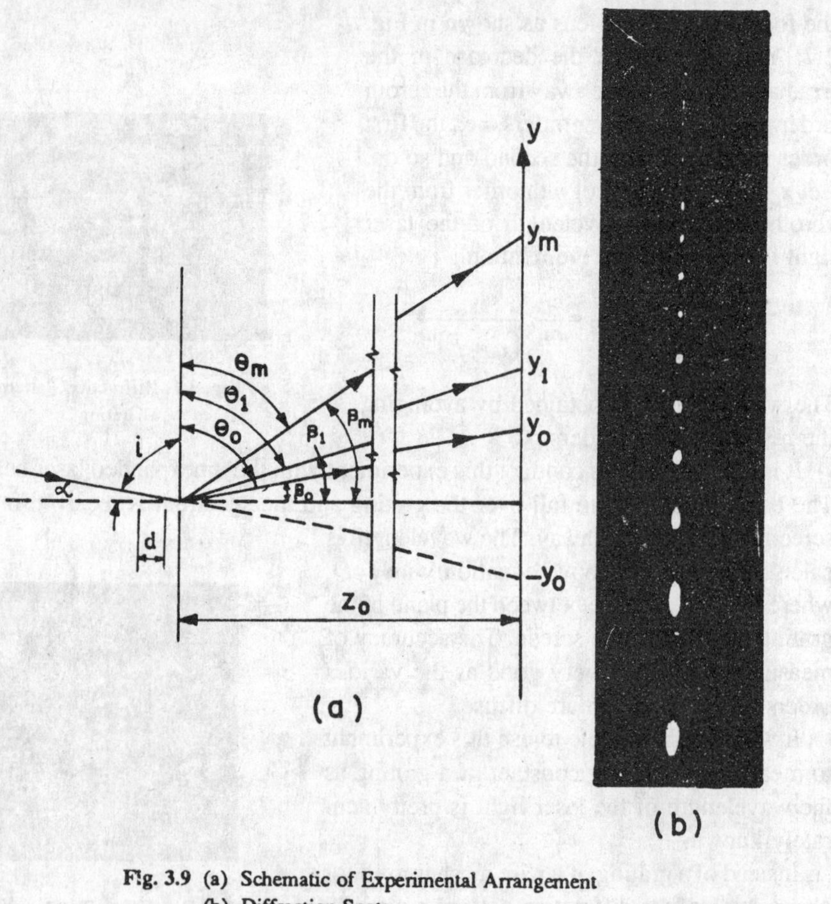


Fig. 3.9 (a) Schematic of Experimental Arrangement
(b) Diffraction Spots

The pattern arises due to the diffraction at the engraving on the scale, and is governed by the grating equation

$$d(\sin i - \sin \theta_m) = m\lambda \tag{3.32}$$

where $m$ is the order and $d$ is the grating constant. For $m = 0$, the beam is specularly reflected. The grating equation is expressed in terms of angles $\alpha$ and $\beta$ in the form

$$d(\cos \alpha - \cos \beta_m) = m\lambda \tag{3.33}$$

where $\alpha = \frac{\pi}{2} - i$ and $\beta_m = \frac{\pi}{2} - \theta_m$.

The distance between the region of incidence at the ruler and the screen is $z_0$. The diffraction spots are taken to lie along *y*-axis, and the position of *m*th spot is represented by $y_m$.

For zeroth order $\alpha = \beta_0$. Therefore

$$\cos \beta_m = \left[1 - (y_m / z_0)^2\right]^{1/2} = 1 - \frac{1}{2} \cdot \frac{y_m^2}{z_0^2} + \ldots \tag{3.34a}$$

Similarly,

$$\cos\alpha = \cos \beta_0 = 1 - \frac{1}{2} \cdot \frac{y_0^2}{z_0^2} + \ldots \tag{3.34b}$$

Therefore,

$$\cos\alpha - \cos \beta_m = \frac{(y_m^2 - y_0^2)}{2 z_0^2} \tag{3.35}$$

The wavelength of the light is thus given by

$$\lambda = \frac{d}{2 z_0^2} \cdot \frac{y_m^2 - y_0^2}{m} \tag{3.36}$$

The distances are measured from the horizontal plane. For this purpose the position of the direct beam (in the absence of the vernier caliper) is marked on the screen, and the distances of various diffraction spots are measured from this position, and later reduced to the position midway between the direct beam and specularly reflected beam positions. These distances can be measured on a millimeter graph paper pasted on the screen. The distance $z_0$ can be measured with a meter scale. An accuracy of better than 2% can be achieved in a hastily performed experiment. With little care wavelength can be measured within 1% of its value.

In an experiment where much care was not exercised, following data was obtained:

$d$=1 mm (spacing of engravings on the scale)
$z_0$ = 4020 mm

| Observations | | | | | |
|---|---|---|---|---|---|
| Sl. No. | Positions of spot, mm | | Reduced positions | $y_m^2$ | $y_m^2 - y_0^2$ |
| 1 | 0 | | 0 | 0 | |
| 2 | 198 | $y_0$ | 99 | 9801 | |
| 3 | 275 | $y_1$ | 176 | 30976 | 21171 |
| 4 | 326 | $y_2$ | 227 | 51529 | 41728 |
| 5 | 367 | $y_3$ | 268 | 71824 | 62023 |
| 6 | 404 | $y_4$ | 305 | 93025 | 83224 |
| 7 | 437 | $y_5$ | 338 | 114244 | 104443 |
| 8 | 467 | $y_6$ | 368 | 135424 | 125623 |
| 9 | 495 | $y_7$ | 396 | 156816 | 147015 |
| 10 | 520 | $y_8$ | 421 | 177241 | 167440 |
| 11 | 543 | $y_9$ | 444 | 197136 | 187335 |
| 12 | 563 | $y_{10}$ | 464 | 215296 | 205495 |

The average value of $\left(y_m^2 - y_0^2\right)/m$ is 20863.8. Therefore, the wavelength λ is given by

$$\lambda = \frac{1}{2} \cdot \frac{20863.8}{4020 \times 4020} = 0.0006455 \text{ mm}$$

The percentage accuracy is approximately 2%. With more care better results can be obtained.

## 3.6 Screw Testing*

Figure 3.10(a) shows a screw of diameter $d$, pitch $p$ and thread angle $\alpha$. When this screw is placed in the collimated beam, its diffraction pattern is displayed at the

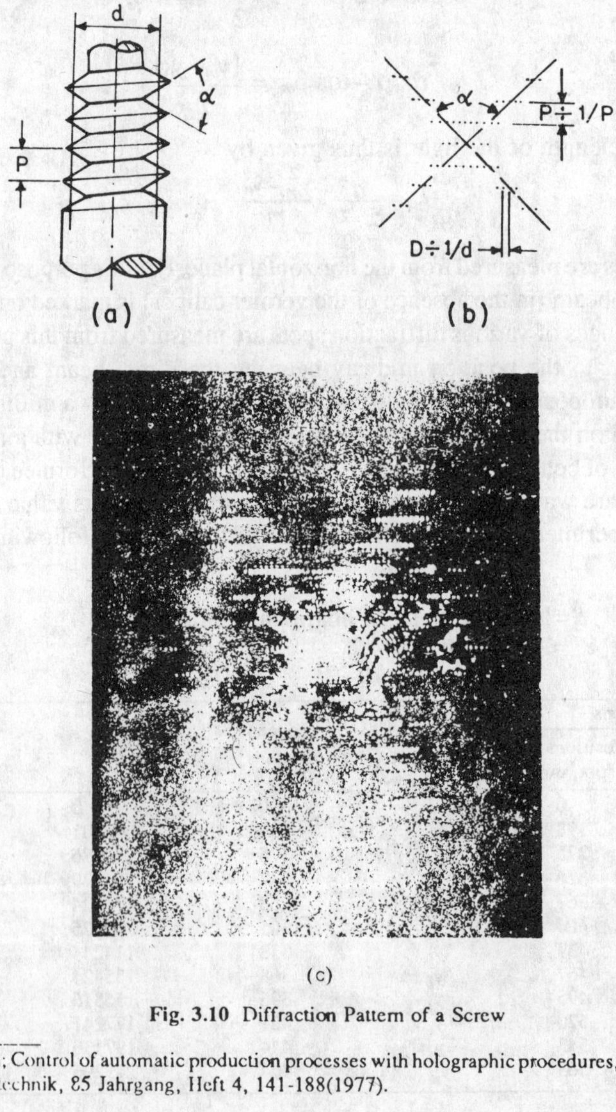


Fig. 3.10 Diffraction Pattern of a Screw

*J. Steffen; Control of automatic production processes with holographic procedures, Feinwerktechnik and Messtechnik, 85 Jahrgang, Heft 4, 141-188(1977).

back focal plane of a lens. A sketch of the diffraction pattern is shown alongside in Fig. 3.10 (b). The pattern is in the form of *X*, and the thread angle can be easily measured from the pattern. The coarse periodicity in the pattern is inversely related to the pitch, while the fine periodicity to the major diameter of the screw.

The intensity distribution at the focal plane of the lens can be obtained following Figs. 3.11(a) and (b). Fig. 3.11(a) shows a section of one pitch of the screw; this is considered as a diffracting aperture. The screw is considered as having *N* such elements.

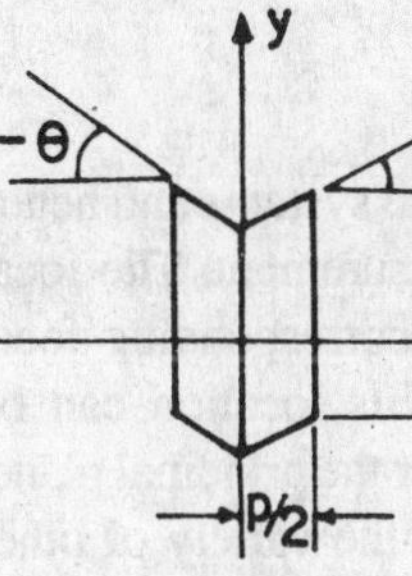

$$f(x, y) = 1 ;\quad 0 < x < p/2 : mx - D/2 < y < mx + D/2$$
$$= 0 \quad \text{Otherwise}$$
$$m = \tan\theta$$

$$I_1(\mu, \nu) = C^2 D^2 p^2/4 \; \text{sinc}^2 (D\nu) \; \text{sinc}^2 \left\{ (\mu + m\nu)\, p/2 \right\}$$

(a)

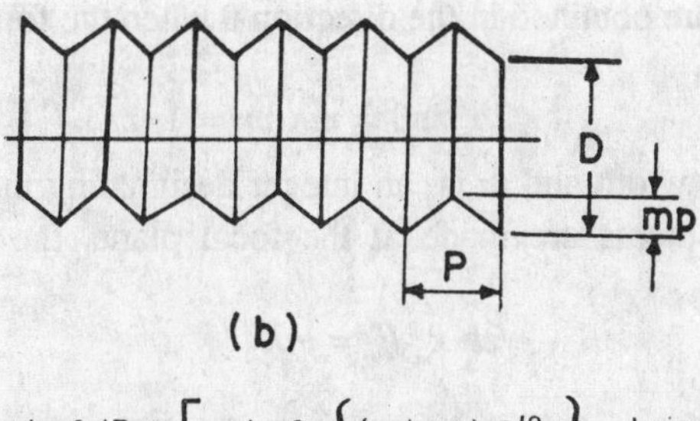

(b)

$$I(\mu, \nu) = C^2 D^2 p^2/4 \; \text{sinc}^2 (D\nu) \Big[ \text{sinc}^2 \left\{ (\mu + m\nu)\, p/2 \right\} + \text{sinc}^2 \left\{ (\mu - m\nu)\, p/2 \right\} + 2\, \text{sinc} \left\{ (\mu + m\nu)\, p/2 \right\} \text{sinc} \left\{ (\mu - m\nu)\, p/2 \right\} \cos (\pi \mu p) \Big] \cdot \frac{\sin^2 (N\pi\mu p)}{\sin^2 (\pi\mu p)}$$

**Fig. 3.11** Calculation of Irradiance Distribution in the Diffraction Pattern of a Screw

If only the parameters of the screw are to be measured the experiment is included under 'Diffraction'. However, using a complementary screen as a filter, the experiment can be modified to test the screws for errors in a production line. The experiment can then be included under 'Coherent Optics'.

**Experiment 3.8:** To measure the thread angle, pitch and the diameter of a micrometer screw.

**Equipments:** A laser with a beam expander, a lens. a micrometer screw, a ground glass plate or a camera.

**Procedure:** The laser beam is expanded and collimated to a diameter of about

25 mm. The micrometer screw, thoroughly cleaned, is placed in the beam with its axis perpendicular to the optic axis. A lens of sufficiently large aperture (> 40 mm) is kept near the screw. The diffraction pattern of the screw will be displayed at the focal plane of the lens. The diffraction pattern can either be taken on the ground glass plate or photographed. Figure 3.10(c) shows a diffraction pattern of a screw. The thread angle, pitch and diameter of the screw can then be calculated from the observation made on the diffraction pattern. The calculations for pitch and diameter require the value of the focal length of the lens.

## 3.7 Measurement of Focal Length

The focal length is a very important parameter of the optical systems and hence a large number of methods have been developed for its measurement. The focal length is the distance between the principal plane and the corresponding focal plane. While the focal plane is physically accessible and its location can be obtained very accurately by a variety of methods, it is not so far the principal plane. Thus the accurate determination of focal length depends on the variety of other properties of the imaging system such as angular magnification, lateral magnification, etc. Here we present a simple method that involves diffraction, and is not influenced by the degree of collimation of the incident beam. The method easily offers accuracy around 1%.

For simplicity we consider diffraction at a single slit. The minima in the diffraction pattern are obtained in the direction θ when the following condition is satisfied:

$$2b \sin\theta = m\lambda \;: m = 1, 2, \ldots \tag{3.37}$$

where $2b$ is the slit width and $m$ is an integer designating the diffraction order. When the measurements are made at the focal plane, the above equation is rewritten as

$$2b\, x_m / f = m\lambda \tag{3.38}$$

where $x_m$ is the position of the $m$th minima in the diffraction pattern. Therefore,

$$f = 2b\,(x_m - x_{m-1})/\lambda \tag{3.39}$$

Higher accuracy is achieved when a linear grating is used instead of a slit as the grating spacing can be experimentally measured with higher accuracy than the slit width and the measurements are made on the maxima which are sharper due to multiple beam interference. The locations of maxima in the diffraction pattern of a linear grating is given by

$$d \sin\theta = m\lambda \;: m = 0, 1, 2, \ldots \tag{3.29}$$

where $d$ is the grating pitch and θ is the direction in which $m$th diffraction maxima is formed. The focal length, under small angle diffraction, is given by

$$f = d\,(x_m - x_{m-1})/\lambda \tag{3.40}$$

The diffraction patterns of a single slit and a grating are shown in Figure 3.2 and 3.7. It may be noted that the method measures focal length of positive lenses only.

**Experiment 3.9:** To measure the focal length of a given lens.

**Equipments:** A laser source, a collimator, a slit/grating, a test lens and a micrometer eyepiece or a travelling microscope.

**Procedure:** The laser beam is expanded and collimated to the required size, usually the size of the test lens. The degree of collimation is not critical. The

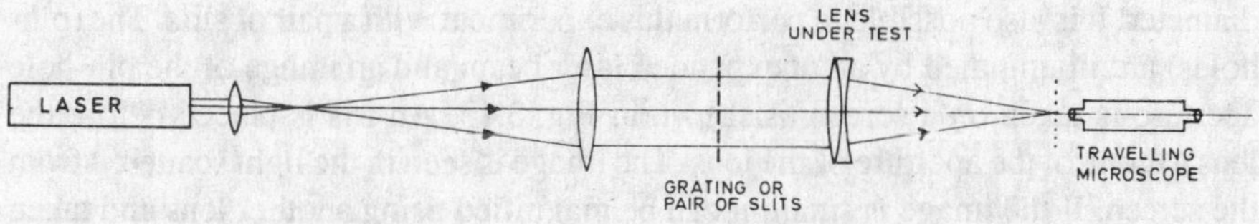


**Fig. 3.12** Measurement of Focal Length

diffracting aperture (slit/grating) is placed in the beam followed by a test lens as shown in Fig. 3.12. Since the experiment involves visual measurements, the laser power should be reduced to a very low level (within the safe limits) by inserting neutral density filters in the beam. Under no circumstances attempt should be made to view the diffraction pattern directly.

The location of minima for slit aperture and of maxima for linear grating are measured with a micrometer eyepiece or a travelling microscope. The average value of $(x_m - x_{m-1})$ is then found. If gratings of different pitches or a variable slit are available, the locations can be measured for different values of $d$ or $b$. The product $d(x_m - x_{m-1})$ or $2b(x_m - x_{m-1})$ is a constant which is equal to $f\lambda$.

The experiment can also be performed using electronic detection. A linear array detector is used. The accuracy is now determined by the pixel spacing. Further the slit or the grating should be placed in such a way that they are perpendicular to the array detector requiring micropositioners for their mountings.

## 3.8 Resolving Power of a Lens

An imaging lens must yield a point image for a point source under geometrical optics. However, due to diffraction, a point object is imaged as a distribution known as Airy distribution. This contains a central disc of angular radius $\lambda/2R$ surrounded by the diffraction rings. Most of the energy is concentrated in the central disc and hence the image of a point is taken as a disc of finite dimension. In practice, a point source can be of finite size.

If we consider two separate point sources, their images will be Airy distributions which may or may not overlap. If the point sources are brought closer, their images will also move nearer to each other. At some point objects separation, the two distributions overlap in such a way that it may be difficult to say that there are two distinct point objects. The objects are then said to be unresolved. On the other hand, the Airy distributions may be sufficiently far apart to unmistakenly say that there are two point objects. The objects are then fully resolved. There is however a criterion, known as Reyleigh criterion, which specifies the condition of just resolution of the point objects. According to Rayleigh criterion, the two objects are just resolved when the first minimum in the diffraction pattern of one object falls on the central maximum of the other object. In other words, the angular separation between the object is equal to the angular radius of the Airy disc (or central maximum).

**Experiment 3.10:** To study the resolving power of an imaging lens.

**Equipments:** A pair of pin-hole aperture plate, He-Ne laser, a test lens with an iris diaphragm and a screen.

**Procedure:** A pair of pin-hole consists of two circular holes say each of 0.1 mm diameter. It is also possible to perform this experiment with a pair of slits. The (pin-holes) are illuminated by an unexpanded laser beam and an image of the pin-hole aperture is taken on a screen as shown in Fig. 3.13. An iris is placed before the lens to control the aperture of the lens. The image is seen in the light scattered from the screen. If the image is small, it can be magnified using another lens and taken on the screen.

Let $p$ be the linear separation between the two point sources, which are placed at a distance $u$ from the lens. The image separation will be $Mp$ where $M$ $(= v/u)$ is the magnification of the imaging lens and $v$ is the image distance. The angular radius of the Airy disc is $1.22\ \lambda/2R$. Therefore, at the condition of just resolution,

$$\frac{1.22\lambda}{2R} = \frac{p}{u} = \frac{Mp}{v} \tag{3.41}$$

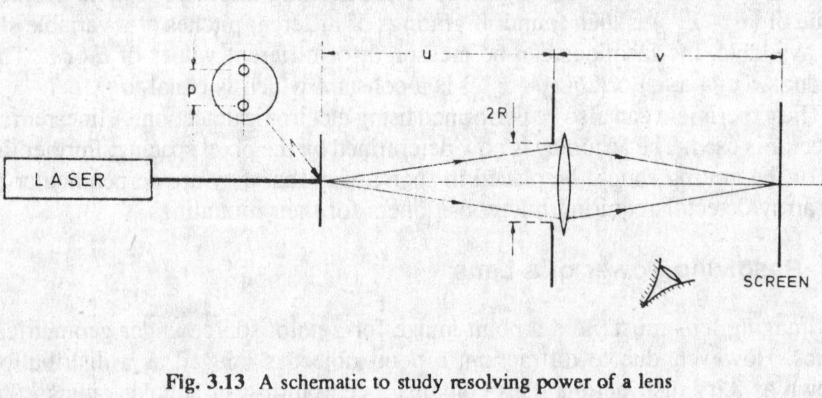


**Fig. 3.13** A schematic to study resolving power of a lens

Thus

$$2R = \frac{1.22\lambda\ u}{p} \tag{3.42}$$

Here $2R$ is the diameter of the lens controlled by the iris aperture for the condition of just resolution. The experiment can be performed for various object distances $u$. A graph between $2R$ and $u$ is a straight line whose slope is related to the separation of object points, which then could be determined.

## PROBLEMS

1. Take a round coin and place it in the collimated beam. What do you obtain at the center of the shadow? Explain your observation.
2. Observe the Fresnel diffraction pattern of a circular aperture. Can you obtain the diameter of the aperture by the study of the pattern?
3. Observe diffraction pattern of a straight edge in the Fresnel region. Explain why the relative irradiances of maxima and minima remain practically constant at all distances from the diffracting edge.
4. Prove that zone plate behaves like a lens. What kind of diffraction pattern do you expect from a zone plate?
5. Prove that two kinds of zone plates, one with the central zone opaque and other transparent, are identical in their optical performance.
6. Calculate the chromatic aberration of a zone plate. Why can not it be achromatized?
7. How do we look for periodicites in a seemingly random pattern?
8. Explain the principle of the method used to control the diameter of the fibre drawn using diffraction of light.
9. Sprinkle lycopodium powder on a glass plate and insert it into a laser beam. What kind of diffraction pattern is observed at a screen placed tens of centimeters away. Can we obtain an average size of the particles from the study of the diffraction pattern?
10. A collimated beam of light containing two wavelengths, 0.52 $\mu m$ and 0.55 $\mu m$, is incident normally on a grating having 3500 lines per centimeter. The diffracted beam is focused on a screen by a long focus lens of focal length of 1.5 meters. Find the distances on the screen in centimeters between the spectral line in (a) first order, and (b) second order.
11. Observe the diffraction pattern of an annular aperture, and compare the pattern with that obtained from corresponding full aperture. Mention some applications of the annular aperture.

# 4. Polarisation of Light

## 4.1 Introduction to Polarisation and Malus Law

The phenomena of interference and diffraction establish a fact that the light is of wave nature but do not indicate the type of the wave—longitudinal or transverse. The eletromagnetic theory, however, specifically requires that the vibrations be transverse, being therefore entirely confined to the plane of the wavefront. Experiments show that light waves possess an asymmetry with respect to the direction of propagation. The longitudinal waves like sound disturbances are symmetrical with respect to the direction of propagation while the transverse waves exhibit asymmetry and are said to be polarised. Transverse nature of light waves comes into play when we consider interaction of light with matter.

Most general kind of polarisation state is elliptical; linear and circular polarisation states being the special cases. The light emitted from thermal sources like incandescent lamps, discharge tubes, etc. is not polarised because the atoms though emit polarised light are independent to each other and hence emit in all polarisation states. Thus over the period of observation it behaves like an unpolarised light. The unpolarised light can be considered to be composed of two linear orthogonal polarisation states with complete incoherence. The output of a laser with Brewster windows is linearly polarised, its orientation is dependent on the orientation of Brewster window with the direction of propagation of the beam.

There are various arrangements to obtain linearly, circularly or elliptically polarised light from the unpolarised natural light. The device which produces linearly polarised light from natural light is called a linear polariser or commonly just a polariser, whereas the devices that produce circularly or elliptically polarised light are known circular or elliptical polarisers. The common examples of linear polarisers are Nicol prism, Glan-Thompson prism, polaroid sheets etc. A combination of a linear polariser and a quarter wave plate at various orientations will act as an elliptical polariser.

A linear polariser has 100% transmission for linearly polarised light of a certain orientation and zero transmission at an orientation orthogonal to it. When a beam of natural light is incident on a polariser, the transmitted beam is linearly polarised with the vibration direction parallel to the transmission axis of the polariser but is of half the irradiance of the incident beam. Any rotation of the polariser changes the orientation of the linearly polarised light but not its irradiance. On the other hand, if a linearly polarised beam is incident on the polariser, the irradiance of the transmitted beam will vary with the rotation of the polariser. Malus law relates the irradiance of the transmitted beam with the orientation of the polariser measured from its transmission axis. The proof of the law rests on a simple fact that any linearly polarised beam may be resolved into two components, one parallel to the transmission axis and the other orthogonal to it. Figure 4.1 illustrates a linearly polarised beam of amplitude $A_0$ with orientation along *OL* incident on a polariser with transmission axis along *OT*. The amplitude $A_1$ of light that passes through the polariser is, therefore,

$$A_l = A_0 \cos\theta$$

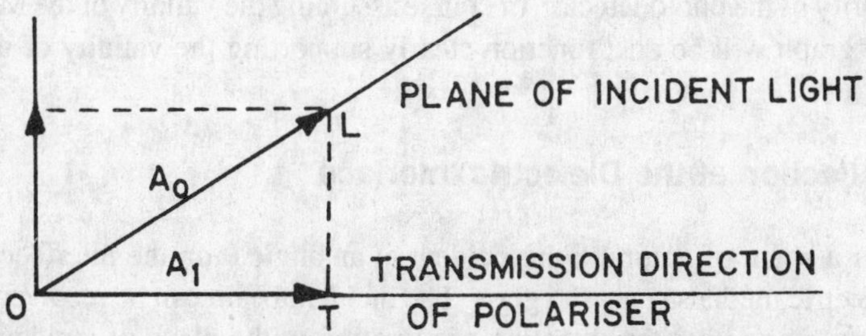


**Fig. 4.1** Illustrating the Malus Law

The irradiance of the transmitted beam is

$$I_1 = I_0 \cos^2\theta, \tag{4.1}$$

where $I_0$ is the irradiance of the incident polarised beam.

The Malus law states that the transmitted irradiance varies as the square of the cosine of the angle between the orientation of the incident linearly polarised light and the transmission axis of the polariser. This law plays an important role in the modulation of light.

**Experiment 4.1:** Verification of the Malus law.

**Equipments:** A He-Ne laser, a polariser in a rotatable mount with graduated scale, a photodetector and an indicating instrument (power meter).

**Procedure:** The experiment can be performed with natural light. However, the laser output is linearly polarised with the vibration direction confined in the vertical plane for most of the commercial units. Further the beam is collimated. If the output of the laser is not polarised; it can be polarised by inserting a polarizer at a proper orientation. The linearly polarised beam is allowed to pass through another polariser fitted on a rotatable mount with a graduated scale as shown in Fig. 4.2. Normally the transmission axis is marked on the bought out polariser assembly. Otherwise it can be marked as it corresponds to the maximum output of the photodetector.

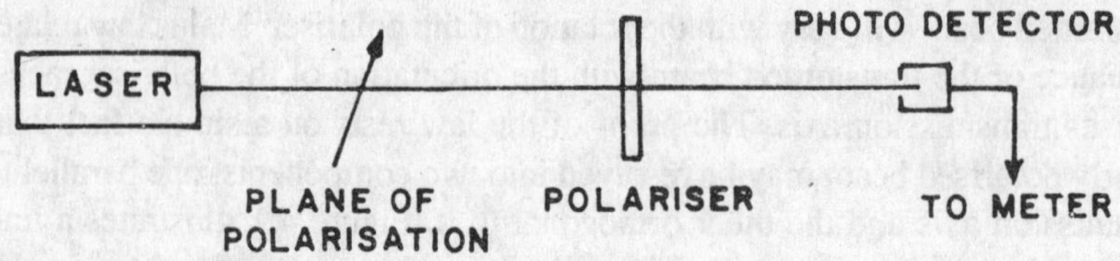


**Fig. 4.2** Verification of the Malus Law

The polariser is rotated in increments of 5° from the position of transmission direction (marked 0°) and the output of the photodetector is read off for all orientations of the polariser between 0° to 180°. A graph between the orientation of the polariser and the output of the photodetector is then drawn. If the response of the photodetector is linear (indeed this experiment can be conducted to check the linearity of the photodetector, of course assuming the validity of the Malus law) then the graph will be $\cos^2$ function clearly supporting the validity of the Malus law.

## 4.2 Reflection at the Dielectric Interface

Consider a beam of natural light incident at an angle θ on the interface between two dielectric media say air and glass. The incident beam can be resolved into two components–one with the direction of vibration in the plane of incidence and is called *p* (parallel) component and other orthogonal to it, and is called *s* (senkrecht) component. According to Electromagnetic theory these components have different reflection coefficients which are functions of angle of incidence except for normal incidence when they are same. The reflected beam is thus partially polarised. However, at a particular angle of incident, called Brewster angle, $\theta_B$, the reflection coefficient for the parallel component is zero, and hence the reflected light has only the *s* component, and it is thus linearly polarised. Brewster discovered that at this angle, the direction of reflected and transmitted beams are 90° apart. Using Snell's law we immediately obtain that

$$\tan \theta_B = n \tag{4.2}$$

where *n* is the refractive index of the dielectric. This is known as Brewster law. The Brewster angle depends on refractive index and hence varies with wavelength. The measurement of Brewster angle is used for obtaining the refractive index, and also for calibrating the polarisers. Since the transmission is 100% for parallel component, Brewster windows in lasers do not introduce any reflection loss. The output of the laser is *p*-polarised, and the direction of vibration can be made vertical by rotating the tube in gas-lasers such that the plane of incidence at the window is horizontal.

The knowledge of Brewster angle is often used to obtain the refractive index of transparent materials. In practice due to contamination of the surface, the reflected beam is weakly elliptically polarised and hence may introduce some error in the measurement of Brewster angle.

**Experiment 4.2:** To measure the Brewster angle and hence the refractive index of a transparent material.

**Equipments:** A He-Ne laser, a plate of transparent material, graduated turn table, a photodetector with indicating instrument.

**Procedure:** The plate of transparent material is mounted on the turn-table such that the plane of incidence is horizontal as shown in Fig. 4.3. In fact, a spectrometer with the eye-piece replaced by a photodetector will be appropriate.

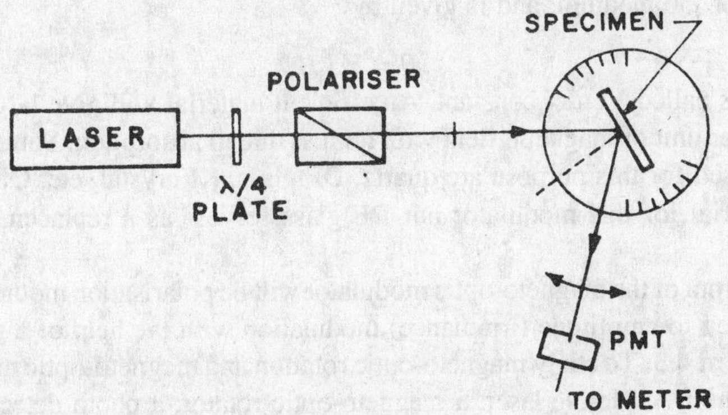


Fig. 4.3 Determination of Brewster Angle

The output of the laser should have its $E$ vector confined to the horizontal plane. The reflected beam as a function of angle of incidence is monitored by the photodetector. The irradiance of the reflected beam can be plotted as a function of angle of incidence. It will be observed that the irradiance keeps on decreasing first, reaches almost zero value and then increases again. The angle at which the irradiance reaches almost zero is the Brewster angle. The refractive index of the plate will be obtained from

$$n = \tan \theta_B$$

## 4.3 Modulation of Light Beam

An important area of application for coherent electromagnetic waves in the optical region involves the technique of transmitting information in the form of modulated beam. The usual methods of modulating the laser beam are frequency modulation, amplitude modulation and phase modulation. The modulation may be internal or external. Internal modulation refers to modulating the signal being generated inside the cavity. External modulation refers to passing the beam through a modulating process. The amplitude modulation is the simplest to perform. The amplitude modulation can be accomplished with the aid of Faraday effect, Kerr effect and Pockel effect. We shall, however, discuss an experiment where modulation is achieved by Faraday effect. This experiment in magneto-optic rotation is both impressive and instructive.

The Faraday effect (magneto-optic rotation) is the rotation of the plane of polarisation of a light wave as it travels through certain materials in a direction parallel to an applied magnetic field. The linearly polarised beam, as it travels through a transparent medium placed in a longitudinal magnetic field, splits into two inverse circularly polarised beams. These beams travel at different velocities in the magnetised medium. On leaving the medium they recombine again producing a linearly polarised beam with its plane of vibration rotated with respect to that of the incident beam.

The angle of rotation $\theta$ depends on the strength of the magnetic field $H$ and the length $l$ of the medium, and is given by

$$\theta = V\,l\,H \tag{4.3}$$

where $V$ is called Verdet constant. An efficient material will give large Faraday rotation per unit of magnetic field with no loss due to absorption. Some materials that are used for this purpose are quartz, DF glass, KI crystal, etc. Quartz is the best material for this modulator but DF glass serves as a replacement at low currents.

The output of the magneto-optic modulator will be polarisation modulated. This is converted to amplitude (irradiance) modulation with the help of a polariser.

**Experiment 4.3:** To study magneto-optic rotation and magneto-optic modulation.

**Equipments:** A He-Ne laser, a magneto-optic rotator, a photo-detector and an indicator or a receiver.

**Procedure:** The experimental arrangement for magneto-optic modulation is shown in Fig. 4.4. The beam from the He-Ne laser is used as the carrier. The modulator is a rod of dense flint glass of a small length and a narrow cross-section, over which a number of turns of insulated copper wire are wound. A polariser is

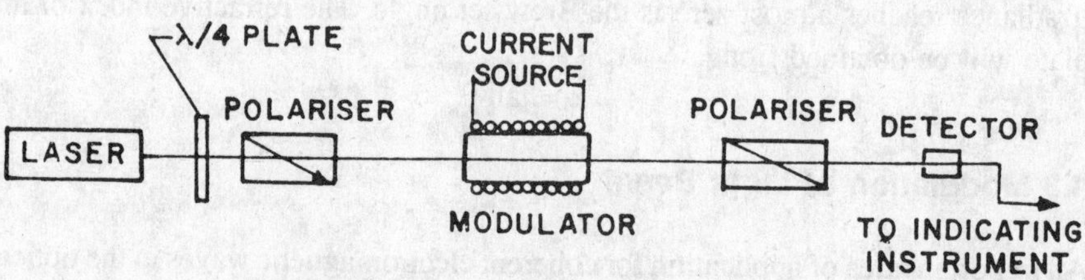


Fig. 4.4 Study of Magneto-Optic Rotation

placed after the modulator. The linearly polarised beam from the laser passes through the modulator, polariser and then is received by the photodetector.

**Static characteristics:** With no current in the modulator winding, the irradiance of light falling on the detector is reduced to minimum by adjusting the position of the polariser. The transmission axis of the polariser is now orthogonal to the orientation of the linear polarisation of the laser beam. As the current is switched on, the magnetic field will rotate the polarisation of the beam, and hence the photodetector will give higher output. The detector output is noted for a number of current values in the modulator windings. The plot between the detector output and the current is highly non-linear. It is of $\cos^2$ type.

If the polariser is kept at 45° with respect to the incident polarisation orientation, the relation between detector output and the current will be linear over a limited range. But there is a very large DC bias, and for static measurements it can not be removed.

**Dynamic characteristics:** On the other hand, if the coil is excited by the amplified signals from an audio source, time varying magnetic field is setup inside the material which serves to modulate the incident beam. The output of the detector, through an a.c. amplifier, is fed to a loudspeaker. Alternately, the coil can be excited by an a.c. current source, and degree of modulation can be studied as a function of frequency. As the modulator winding offers high impedance for high frequencies, the output signal starts falling. Tlhe bandwidth of the magneto-optic modulator is low compared to that of an electro-optic modulator.

## PROBLEMS

1. The effective irradiance of a source is reduced by the use of a polariser and an analyser whose relative orientation is θ. To what accuracy, must θ (in degrees) be known to obtain an accuracy of 2% in the irradiance of the transmitted light at a setting which reduces the irradiance in a ratio of 1:7?
2. In a laser cavity insert a thin glass plate between the mirror and the Brewster window. Observe the output as the glass plate is rotated and brought parallel to the Brewster plate. Obtain experimentally the angular deviation from the Brewster angle for which the laser output does not drop by more than 5%.
3. What angle of rotation in the Faraday effect would be produced by a single traverse of the beam in a block of crown glass ($V$=0.0161 at 18°C) 12 cm. long situated in a magnetic field of 8,000 oersteds?
4. Bring out the differences between Kerr and Faraday effects and mention their applications.
5. Design an optical isolator based on the principle of Faraday rotation.
6. Faraday rotation can be used to measure current in high voltage transmission lines. Design an experimental set up for this purpose.

# 5. Holography

When a wave illuminates an object, transmitted or diffusely reflected wave is modulated both in amplitude and phase. A record of both amplitude and phase will be a complete record of the wave from the object and hence the object itself. All-known recording media in optical region respond to the energy, i.e., absolute amplitude squared and hence the phase information is completely lost. The recording of both the amplitude and phase of the object wave by a square-law detector is accomplished through the phenomenon of interference. A reference wave coherent to the object wave is added at the plane of the recording medium. Both the amplitude and phase of the object wave are recorded as irradiance variations due to interference. Such an interference record is called a hologram; a complete record. Subsequent illumination of the hologram with a reference wave will reconstruct the object wave. On reconstruction, the object with full perspective will be seen in the direction of the object through the hologram although it has since been removed. The holography is thus a two step process:

1. recording of both the amplitude and phase of the object wave on a square-law detector, and
2. reconstruction of the original wave from the hologram.

Therefore, holography is fundamentally different from photography. Three dimensionality and other characteristics exhibited by the holographic image are the consequences of the recording of phase of the object wave.

## 5.1 Recording of a Hologram and Reconstruction

### *Recording*

Let $\hat{a} = a_0 e^{i\phi_a}$ be the amplitude distribution of the object wave at the recording plane. A reference wave $\hat{r} = r_0 e^{i\phi_r}$, coherent to $\hat{a}$, is added at the recording plane as shown in Fig. 5.1 (a). The resultant amplitude distribution is, therefore, given by

$$H = \hat{a} + \hat{r} \tag{5.1}$$

Let us assume that the photographic emulsion is used as a recording medium. The photographic plate will respond to the irradiance distribution. The irradiance distribution is given by

$$I = a_0^2 + r_0^2 + \hat{a}\hat{r}^* + \hat{a}^*\hat{r}$$

$$= a_0^2 + r_0^2 + 2a_0 r_0 \cos(\phi_a - \phi_r). \tag{5.2}$$

Both the amplitude and phase have been recorded as the irradiance variations in the interference pattern. The amplitude $a_0$ modulates the contrast and phase $\phi$ determines the position of the fringes.

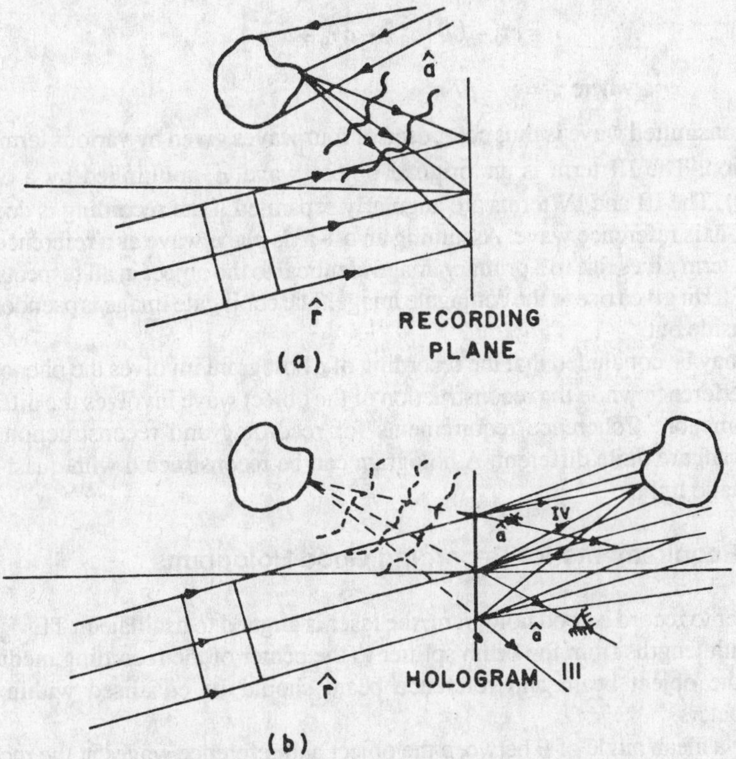


**Fig. 5.1** (a) Recording and (b) Reconstruction of a Wave

The photographic plate is now processed (developed and fixed). The processed plate, having an interference record, is called a hologram. For the sake of simplicity, we assume that the exposure time, $T$, while recording the hologram is such that its amplitude transmittance $\hat{t}$ is proportional to the exposure $E(= IT)$. The hologram provides a linear mapping between the irradiance variations before exposure to the amplitude variations after processing. Thus the amplitude transmittance may be expressed as

$$\hat{t} = t_0 - \beta E = t_0 - \beta IT \tag{5.3}$$

where $\beta$ is a constant of the photographic plate and is negative for negative transparency and positive for positive transparency and $t_0$ is the bias transmittance. If the relation between $\hat{t}$ and $E$ is not linear, higher order images are also formed.

## Reconstruction

The hologram is illuminated with a wave identical to the reference wave. The amplitude of the transmitted wave just after the hologram is given by [Fig. 5.1 (b)]

$$\hat{h} = \hat{t}\hat{r}$$

or

$$\hat{h} = \hat{r}t_0 - \beta T\left[a_0^2\hat{r} + r_0^2\hat{r} + \hat{a}r_0^2 + \hat{a}^*\hat{r}^2\right]$$
$$= \hat{r}t_0' - \beta T\left[a_0^2\hat{r} + \hat{a}r_0^2 + \hat{a}^*\hat{r}^2\right] \tag{5.4}$$

where $t_0' = t_0 - \beta T r_0^2$

The transmitted wave is thus composed of four waves given by various terms in the equation. The III term is an original object wave $\hat{a}$ multiplied by a constant $(\beta T r_0^2)$. The III and IV terms are angularly separated if the recording is done with an off-axis reference wave. Assuming an off-axis plane wave as a reference wave, the III term gives rise to a primary image identical to the object in all respects, while the IV term gives rise to the conjugate image. The conjugate image is pseudoscopic, i.e., inside out.

It may be concluded that the recording of a hologram involves the phenomenon of interference while the reconstruction of the object wave involves the diffraction phenomenon. Coherence requirements for recording and reconstruction of the hologram are quite different. A hologram can be reconstructed with quasi-monochromatic light.

## 5.2 Requirements for Recording Good Holograms

In order to record a good hologram, the laser is aligned to oscillate in $TEM_{00}$ mode and path lengths from the beam splitter to the center of the recording medium for both the object beam and reference beam should be equalised within a few centimeters.

For a mean angle of θ between the object and reference waves at the recording medium, fringes of spatial frequency of sin θ/λ are formed. This calls for high resolution photographic emulsions. These emulsions tend to be extremely slow requiring long exposure time for hologram recording. The path difference change between the object and reference waves due to any external influence, such as vibration, thermal or acoustical, etc. should not exceed by more than λ/8 during the exposure time. The setup is arranged on a table which is isolated from vibrations and other disturbances. In practice it is found that a stone slab weighing about half a ton and supported on 4" thick coir mattress is quite satisfactory. The pneumatic damping is also very effective and hence the stone slab can be supported on inflated tubes.

The ratio of the irradiances of reference wave to object wave at the hologram plane should lie between 3 to 15 in order to have linear recording.

**Experiment 5.1:** Recording of a hologram and reconstruction of the image.

**Equipments:** A gas laser (1 to 10 mW), two microscope objectives, one beam-splitter, two front coated plane mirrors, a plate/film holder, holographic plate/film and processing facilities.

**Procedure:** There are many ways to record a hologram. We shall, however, describe a procedure which is followed by us. Various optical components are mounted on the holographic table as shown in Fig. 5.2. It is not necessary to mount the laser on this table, only the components from the beam-splitter onwards should be on the vibration isolation table. Care should be taken to match the path lengths *ABCD* and *AED*. The beam-splitter divides the beam into two parts: the beam 1 is used as a reference and the beam 2 is used to illuminate the object as shown in Fig. 5.2. The beam 2 should be stronger that the beam 1 as the scattered field from

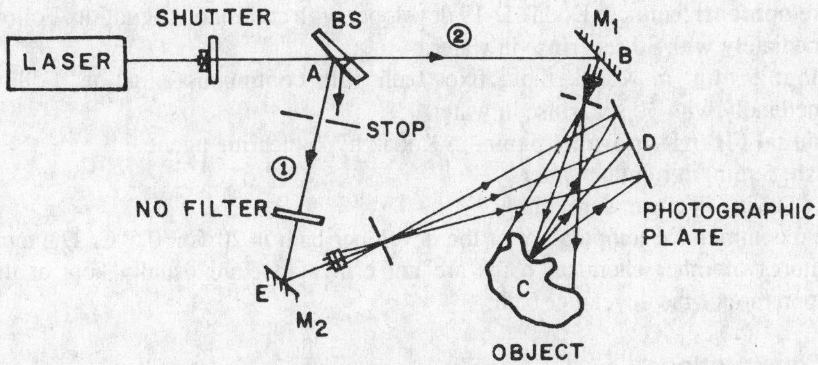


**Fig. 5.2** Schematic of Recording a Hologram

the object is usually very weak. The reflected beam from the second surface of the beam splitter which also goes in the direction of beam 1 can be eliminated by inserting a stop in the path. Use of wedge type beam splitter would be convenient. The mirrors $M_1$ and $M_2$ are used to fold the paths. It may be noted that the beam splitter, mirrors $M_1$ and $M_2$ need not be of good optical quality as the laser beam of approximately 1 mm diameter is incident on them. A pin-hole and microscope objective combination, often called a spatial filter, is inserted in both the beams. The spatial filter removes the high frequency contents in the beam which could arise due to diffraction from dust particles on the optical elements and the spurious interference fringes. The pin-hole of approximately 20$\mu m$ diameter is used. Since the microscope objective focuses the beam at pin-hole, a very accurate alignment of pin-hole and microscope objective is required. The pin-hole is provided with a *x-y* motion and the microscope objective with z-motion. The beam 1 emerging from the spatial filter constitutes a spherical reference wave. The beam 2 from the spatial filter illuminates the object. The beam scattered from the object constitutes the object wave. The irradiances of these two beams are compared at the recording plane. The reference wave must be stronger than the object wave, a ratio of three is normally used, though a ratio up 15 gives reasonable results. A control on the irradiance of the reference wave can be exercised by inserting a variable density filter or a polaroid filter in the beam 1. The object could be any three dimensional diffuse scene; a pair of diffusely reflecting figurine will be a suitable object.

The experiment is carried out in dark. The laser beam is suitably blocked and the photographic plate is inserted in the plate holder which is rigidly mounted on the table. The plate cover is now removed and a few minutes are allowed for the disturbance to subside before the exposure is made by letting the beam remotely. With a 5 mW laser and a diffuse object 20 cm away from the plate, an exposure time of the order of a few seconds is required. If the powers of the beams at the plane of the photographic plate are measured, the exposure time is calculated from the technical data of the plate emulsion supplied by the manufacturer. After the proper exposure has been given, the laser beam is blocked and the plate is removed to the dark room for processing.

**Processing:** Following procedure yields satisfactory results for Kodak and Agfa Gevaert emulsions.

**Development:** 5 min. in Kodak D-19 developer with continuous agitation. Follow immediately with 30 sec. rinse in water.

**Fixing:** 5 min. in Kodak rapid fixer bath with continuous agitation. Follow immediately with 30 sec. rinse in water.

**Residual Fixer Removal:** 1.5 min. in Kodak hypo clearing agent.

**Wash:** 5 min. in running water.

**Dry:** Drying in clean warm air.

The recommended temperature of the developer bath is 20°C ± 0.5°C. The temperatures of other chemical baths are not critical but are usually kept at the temperature of the developer bath.

## Reconstruction

The hologram is mounted back where it was for recording. It is now illuminated only with the reference wave, i.e., the object is removed and beam 2 blocked. On looking through the hologram in the direction of the object one sees the object, as through a window exactly at the same location, although it has since long been removed. By changing the direction of viewing, different perspectives of the image can be seen and photographed. In Fig. 5.3 a photograph of a reconstructed image is given. It may be advisable to reconstruct the image using a spectral lamp as accidental viewing in the direction of the reference wave may be injurious to the eye when laser light is used for reconstruction.

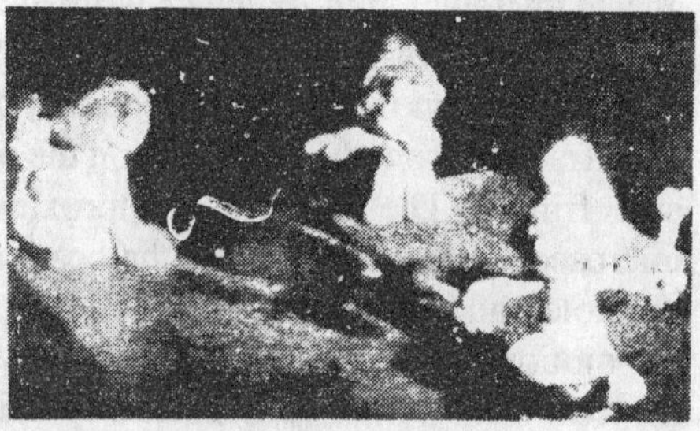

**Fig. 5.3** Photograph of a Reconstructed Image

## 5.3 Phase Holograms

We characterise photosensitive materials as (a) amplitude modulating or absorption materials when the absorption coefficient is exposure dependent, and (b) phase modulating or phase materials when either the refractive index or the thickness is exposure-dependent.

When the interference fringes are recorded as a spatial modulation of absorption coefficient, the hologram is an absorption hologram. The recording of an absorption hologram has been described earlier in detail. When the interference fringes are recorded as a spatial variation of either the refractive index or the thickness or both, the hologram is called a phase hologram. The techniques of recording a phase hologram and subsequent reconstruction of the wave are similar to those of an absorption hologram.

In fact an absorption hologram recorded on a photographic emulsion can be converted into a phase hologram. The conversion involves a chemical bleaching of the emulsion. An effective bleach process for obtaining a high resolution phase hologram is one in which the developed silver in the absorption hologram is replaced by a transparent silver salt with refractive index generally greater than that of the gelatin base. Bleaches containing potassium ferricynide are among the best, they produce stable holograms exhibiting high diffraction efficiency and relatively low noise. One simple procedure to bleach the hologram using this oxydiser is given below:

**Development:** 5 min. in Kodak D-76 developer with continuous agitation. Follow with 30 sec. rinse in water.

**Fixing:** 5 min. in Kodak rapid fixer. Follow with 30 sec. rinse in water.

**Residual Fixer Removal:** 1.5 min. in Kodak hypo clearing agent.

**Wash:** 5 min. in running water.

**Bleach:** 3 min. in 5% aqueous solution of $K_3Fe(CN)_6$.

**Wash:** 5 min. in running water.

**Dry:** With clean warm air.

Alternatively a dry bleach process using Bromine vapour can be used. The phase holograms exhibit high diffraction efficiency. Theoretical diffraction efficiency for thin phase holograms is 33.9% as against of 6.25% for thin absorption holograms. The diffraction efficiency of thick phase hologram may approach 100%; the images reconstructed from phase holograms are, therefore, brighter. The phase holograms are non-linear due to their very nature and hence produce higher order images. In general, there is greater scattering from the phase holograms compared to the absorption holograms which results in noise in the images.

**Experiment 5.2:** To fabricate a grating and a zone plate.

**Apparatus:** A He-Ne laser, a pair of good quality mirrors, a pair of beam splitters, an achromate and holographic plates.

**Procedure:**

**Fabrication of a grating:**

A grating is a periodic structure and the simplest way to make a grating is to record an interference pattern of two plane waves. The laser beam is, therefore, expanded and collimated (Fig. 5.4). The collimated beam is divided into two beams with the beam splitter BS which are folded by mirrors $M_1$ and $M_2$. The photographic plate is placed in the region of superposition. The region of superposition can be easily checked by inserting a white paper in the beam, and looking for the superposition region. An appropriate exposure is given to the plate which on development would

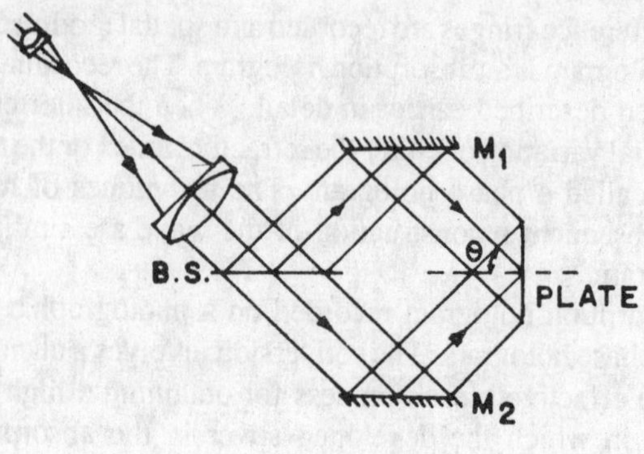


**Fig. 5.4 Schematic for Fabricating a Plane Grating Holographically**

be a diffraction grating. If the angle between two beams is $2\theta$, and the holographic plate is symmetrically placed, the grating pitch $d$ is given by

$$d = \frac{\lambda}{2 \sin \theta} \tag{5.5}$$

In practice it may be difficult to maintain the constancy of angle $\theta$ over longer periods. Hence either a wedge plate or a bi-mirror arrangement is used. If the angle of the wedge is $\alpha$ and a collimated beam is incident at an angle $\theta_i$ at its front surface, the angle $2\theta$ between the two collimated beams, one reflected from the front and other from the back surface of the plate, is given by

$$2\theta = \theta_i - \sin^{-1}[\sin \theta_i \cos 2\alpha - (n^2 - \sin^2\theta_i)^{1/2} \sin 2\alpha] \tag{5.6}$$

where $n$ is the refractive index of the plate. For small angle of the wedge such that $\cos 2\alpha \sim 1$ and $\sin 2\alpha \sim 2\alpha$, the angle $2\theta$ is given by

$$2\theta = \sin^{-1}[2\alpha(n^2 - \sin^2\theta_i)^{1/2}] \tag{5.7}$$

When a bi-mirror arrangement with an enclosed angle of $(\pi - \alpha)$ is used, the two reflected beams contain an angle of $2\alpha$. This arrangement is insensitive to the change in the angle of incidence. The photographic plate is placed at the region of overlap of the two beams.

**Fabrication of a zone plate:**

A grating that is obtained by recording an interference pattern between a spherical wave and a plane wave is a sinusoidal zone plate. A schematic for recording a zone plate is shown in Fig. 5.5. It is a Mach-Zehnder interferometer; an arm of which has an achromat. The achromat focusses the plane wave at $F$. The holographic plate records interference between a divergent spherical wave from F and a plane wave. The phase factor of the divergent wave at the holographic plate is $\exp\{ik(x^2+y^2)/2f\}$ where $f$ is the distance between $F$ and the plane of the plate. On development, the plate will act as a lens which will bring a collimated beam to focus at a distance of

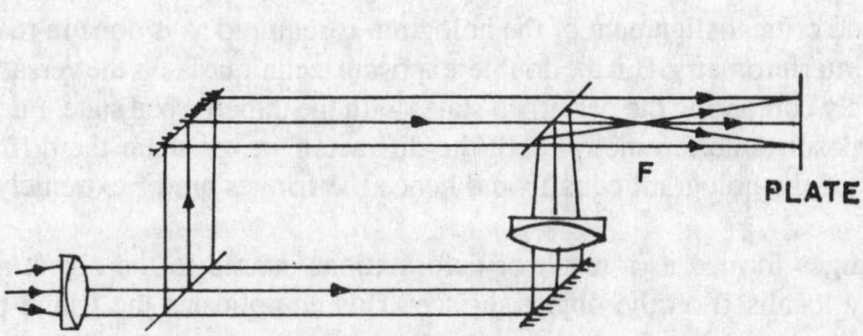


**Fig. 5.5** Schematic for Fabricating a Zone Plate

*f*. In fact it behaves as a divergent lens as well. If the plate is over exposed and bleached it would exhibit multi-foci at $f, f/2, f/3$....

## 5.4 Hologram Interferometry

It was realised in 1965 by a number of investigators that the wavefronts separated both in time and space can interfere with each other. The awareness of this fact gave rise to a new branch of interferometry; which is called hologram interferometry.

It is well-known that when a properly located hologram is illuminated with the reference wave, an object wave is generated producing an image identical with the object at the same location. If the object is also present and illuminated, then two waves, one from the object and transmitted through the hologram, and another released from the hologram, are produced. If the object has not been perturbed, both these waves are identical in all respects but for the amplitude and will interfere to produce a null condition. The null condition arises due to a phase change of $\pi$ on processing of the hologram. However, any perturbation of the object will result in the appearance of fringes which are representative of the perturbation. The dark fringes occur when

$$\phi'_a - \phi_a = 2m\pi, \quad m = 0, \pm 1, \pm 2 \ldots \tag{5.8}$$

where $\phi'_a$ and $\phi_a$ are the phases of the waves from perturbed and unperturbed object respectively. Any perturbation in the object will simultaneously result in the change of fringe pattern and hence the method is called 'real-time hologram interferometry'. It is sometimes called as live-fringe or single-exposure hologram interferometry.

Another possibility also exists for the comparison of two states of the object. This is called 'frozen-fringe' or 'double-exposure' hologram interferometry. In this method a record of the object wave is made. The object is now perturbed and a second record on the same plate is made, i.e., two events in succession are recorded on the plate. After processing, the hologram is illuminated with the reference wave. The waves corresponding to the perturbed and unperturbed states of the object are generated. These waves interfere producing fringes characteristic of the deformation. The condition of interference for the bright fringes is given by

$$\phi'_a - \phi_a = 2m\pi \tag{5.9}$$

Note that no critical alignment of the hologram is required as is done in real-time hologram interferometry. But the double-exposure technique lacks the versatility of continuously comparing the perturbed states with the unperturbed state. Further in double-exposure interferometry, both the diffracted waves share the diffraction efficiency of the hologram equally and hence the fringes are of extremely good contrast.

The fringes formed as a result of deformations caused to the object are not necessarily localised on the object surface. This complicates the fringe pattern analysis. However, when the directions of illumination and observation are at right angle to each other, the fringes are localised on or very near to the object surface. Thus a low power viewing system is used for analysing the fringe pattern or a camera with a large depth of field is used to photograph the fringe pattern. Multiple holograms in different directions of observation of the object have been recorded to analyse three dimensional deformation.

## 5.5 Measurement of Young's Modulus

Young's modulus of a material can be calculated using deflection equation of a cantilever. The deflection equation of the cantilever is given by

$$\Delta z = \frac{PL^3}{3EI} \tag{5.10}$$

where $P$ is the load in Kg, $L$ is the effective span in cm, $E$ is the Young's modulus in Kgf/cm$^2$, $I$ is the moment of inertia in cm$^4$, and $\Delta z$ is the deflection at $L$ in cm.

The moment of inertia can be obtained from the physical dimensions of the cantilever. Its value for a rectangular beam of width $a$ and thickness $b$ is $ab^3/12$.

The above equation is rewritten to give the value of Young's modulus as

$$E = \frac{PL^3}{3I\Delta z}$$

The value of deflection $\Delta z$ is measured using hologram interferometry. As has been pointed out earlier, hologram interferometry can be applied to any material irrespective of its surface structure, and hence it is applied for the determination of elastic constants of any material.

Let $\theta_i$ and $\theta_0$ be the angles defining the directions of illumination and observation respectively and measured as shown in Fig. 5.6(a). The path difference $\Delta$ between two rays scattered from the two identical points on the object is given by

$$\Delta = \Delta z\, n(\cos\theta_i + \cos\theta_0) \tag{5.11}$$

where $n$ is the refractive index, usually 1 for air. If there are $N$ fringes produced upto the span length $L$ of the cantilever counted from the fixed end, then

$$\Delta = N\lambda \tag{5.12}$$

and hence

$$\Delta z = \frac{N\lambda}{\cos\theta_i + \cos\theta_0} \tag{5.13}$$

Substituting the value of $\Delta z$ from Eq.(5.10) into Eq.(5.13), the value of Young's modulus is given as

$$E = \frac{PL^3(\cos\theta_i + \cos\theta_o)}{3IN\lambda} \tag{5.14}$$

**Experiment 5.3:** To determine the Young's modulus of a given material, say aluminium.

**Equipments:** Holographic set up including a laser, a test piece (an aluminium strip), a loading device, photographic plates and processing facilities.

**Procedure:** The aluminium strip is rigidly mounted on a frame which is fixed on the holographic table. To the free end of the cantilever is tied a string which is taken over a pulley for vertical loading. Initial loading of a few grams weight may prove advantageous for further experimentation. Figure 5.6(a) shows a schematic of the experimental setup.

An exposure using the method described earlier is made. Then a load of a few grams is added in the loading device, and a second exposure on the same plate is made. The hologram thus formed has, therefore, recorded two states of the cantilever. When it is illuminated with the reference wave, a set of fringes superposed on the object is seen; a photograph of the reconstructed image is given in Fig. 5.6(b). The test piece, an aluminium strip, is of 15 x 4 x 0.2 cm³ dimensions

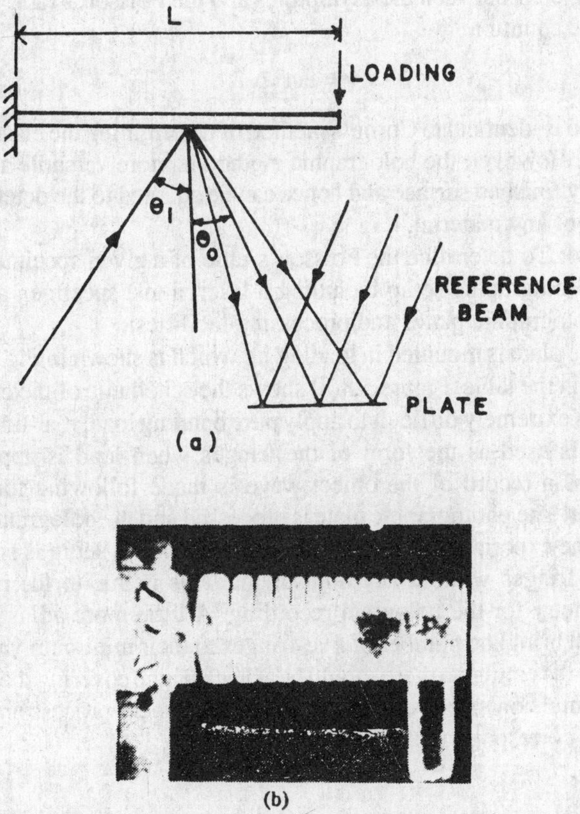


**Fig. 5.6** (a) Recording of a Double Exposure Hologram of a Cantilever, and (b) An Interferogram

with an effective span of 12 cm. The load is 19 mg. The calculated value of $E$ is $0.604 \times 10^6$ Kgf/cm$^2$ which is in very good agreement with the reported value. For the calculation of $E$, mean values of $\theta_i$ and $\theta_0$ are used which can be obtained from the geometry.

## 5.6 Determination of Poisson's Ratio*

The theory of elasticity in three dimensions gives the deformation $u$ of a plate surface after pure bending as

$$u = \frac{x^3 - v^2 (y^2 + b^2/4)}{2R} + \text{constant} \tag{5.15}$$

where $R$ is the radius of curvature of the plate after bending, $v$ the Poisson's ratio of plate material and $b$ its thickness. The origin of co-ordinates is taken at the centroid of the cross-section and $y$-$z$ plane is the plane of bending. Therefore, contour lines of the surface of deformations are hyperbolas with asymptotes given by

$$x^2 - v^2 y^2 = 0 \tag{5.16}$$

The smaller angle $2\alpha$ between the asymptotes and the Poisson's ratio $v$ are related according to the equation

$$v = \tan^2 \alpha \tag{5.17}$$

Thus the method is identical to Cornu's method of determining the elastic constants of a glass plate. However, the holographic method is more versatile as it does not require optically finished surface and hence can be adapted to the determination of Poisson's ratio of any material.

**Experiment 5.4:** To determine the Poisson's ratio of a given specimen.

**Equipments:** Holographic setup including a laser, a test specimen along with a loading jig, photographic plates and processing facilities.

**Procedure:** The plate is mounted in loading jig which is shown in Fig. 5.7. The jig is firmly fixed on the table. Figure 5.8(a) shows the schematic of the experimental setup. Since it is extremely difficult to apply pure bending load, real-time hologram interferometry is used as the form of the fringes when load is applied can be monitored. Thus a record of the object wave is made following the procedure described earlier. The photographic plate is processed and the hologram is mounted in its place in the experimental setup. The geometry of the setup is such that one would see live-fringes without any adjustment. This is due to the near Fourier transform geometry for the hologram recording. A little more adjustment of the plate-holder will bring the number of live-fringes to their minimum value. If there is no swelling of the emulsion there should be a black fringe covering the entire field. However, the emulsion swells due to the wet development process and hence the residual fringes correspond to this effect.

---

*R. Jones and D. Bijl: A holographic interferometric study of the end effects associated with four point bending technique for measuring Poisson's ratio. *J. Phys. E: Sci. Instru.* 7, 357-8(1974).

**Fig. 5.7** Jig for Determination of Poisson's Ratio

The object is now loaded by turning the screws in the jig. If the loading is uniform, hyperbola fringes would be seen in the field while looking through the hologram in the direction of the object. The live-fringe hologram interferometry helps in bringing a right sort of fringe pattern in the field by loading the plate while looking through the hologram, even though the loading jig may not be very good. Further it helps to find out the magnitude of proper load for double-exposure hologram interferometry.

The fringes are not localized at the surface of the plate and hence the camera with low aperture is used to photograph both the object and the fringe pattern. A photograph of the reconstructed image from a double-exposure hologram of a plate of a composite material of dimensions 15 x 4 x 0.4 $cm^3$ and effective span of 13.5 cm is shown in Fig. 5.8(b). The smaller angle of the hyperbola fringes can be measured from the photograph and the Poisson's ratio is calculated from Eq. (5.17).

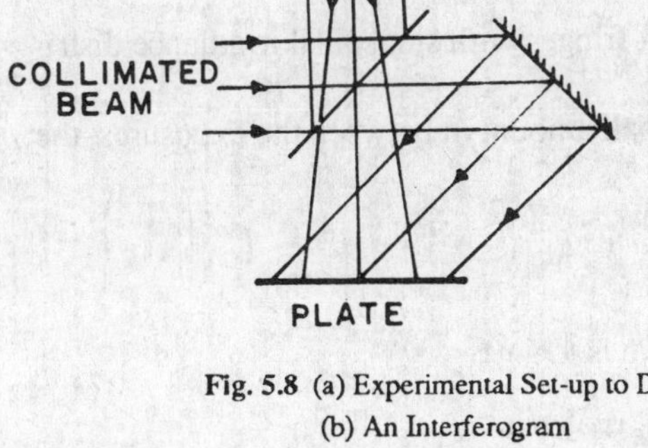


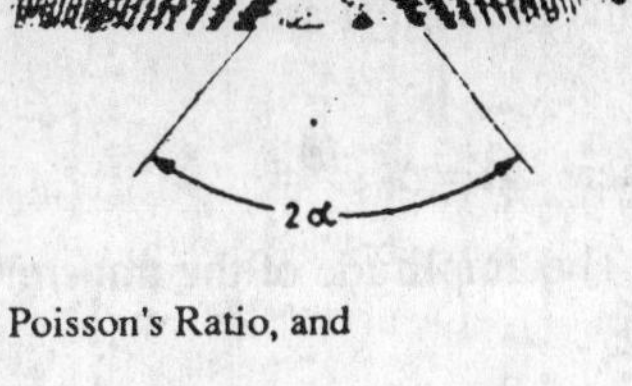


**Fig. 5.8** (a) Experimental Set-up to Determine Poisson's Ratio, and (b) An Interferogram

## 5.7 Measurement of Small Displacements

Some times it may be required to measure displacements which are much smaller than the wavelength of light used. The hologram interferometry either in live-fringe or frozen-fringe mode provides only either a dark field or a bright field. There are, however, many methods to bring out these small path variations into a measurable quantity. We describe a technique known as back-ground fringe technique which can be used to measure very small deformations. The reference beam is angularly displaced between the exposures. Assuming double-exposure interferometry, let us write an expression for the first exposure as

$$E_1 = a_0^2 + r_0^2 + \hat{a}\hat{r}^* + \hat{a}^*\hat{r} \tag{5.18}$$

where $\hat{a} = a_o e^{i\phi_a}$ and $\hat{r} = r_o e^{2\pi i \xi x}$.

The spatial frequency $\xi$ is given by $\xi = \dfrac{\sin\theta}{\lambda}$

The reference beam is a plane wave with a carrier frequency $\xi$. The second exposure is made with a slightly displaced reference wave. The exposure $E_2$ is given by

$$E_2 = a_0^2 + r_0^2 + \hat{a}\hat{r}'^* + \hat{a}^*\hat{r}' \tag{5.19}$$

where $\hat{r}' = r_0 e^{2\pi i \xi' x}$ and $\xi' = \xi \pm \Delta\xi$.

The Total exposure $E$ is given by

$$E = E_1 + E_2 = 2a_0^2 + 2r_0^2 + \hat{a}\left(\hat{r}^* + \hat{r}'^*\right) + \hat{a}^*\left(\hat{r} + \hat{r}'\right)$$

Assuming operation in linear $t$—$E$ region and picking terms of interest from the transmittance expression, the amplitude of the transmitted wave is given by

$$A = \hat{a}\, r_0^2 \left(1 + e^{\pm 2\pi i \Delta\xi x}\right)$$

The irradiance distribution is given by

$$I = |A|^2 = 4a_0^2 r_0^4 \cos^2(\pi\Delta\xi x)$$

Thus the object is covered by straight fringes with sinusoidal irradiance distribution.

If the object is also deformed by a small amount in between the exposures, the terms of interest are

$$= \hat{a}\hat{r}^* + \hat{a}'\hat{r}'^*$$

where $\hat{a}' = a_0 e^{i\phi'_a}$.

The amplitude of the transmitted wave is

$$A = \hat{a}\, r_0^2 \left(1 + e^{\pm 2\pi i \Delta\xi x + i(\phi_a - \phi'_a)}\right)$$

The irradiance distribution is now given by

$$I = 4\,a_o^4\,r_o^2 \cos^2\left(\pi\Delta\xi x + \frac{(\phi_a - \phi_a)}{2}\right)$$

Thus the straight fringes on the object have been modulated due to the deformations of the object.

However, it should be noted that for small deformations, it is desirable to have reference surface with respect to which the deformations are measured. The method thus is extremely suitable and powerful for planar objects.

**Experiment 5.5:** To measure small deformations.

**Equipments:** Holographic setup including a laser, a test object, photographic plates and processing facilities.

**Procedure:** The schematic of the setup is similar to that explained earlier. A glass wedge plate is inserted in the collimated reference beam. The wedge is mounted in such a way that the direction of maximum slope makes an angle of 45° with the vertical. The first exposure is then recorded in the usual way. The wedge is rotated about the direction of laser beam by $\pi/2$ and the object is very minutely deformed. The second exposure is then recorded.

On reconstruction one observes background fringes due to the two different positions of the reference beam as obtained by positioning the wedge. The object deformations modify these fringes.

## PROBLEMS

1. Can you reconstruct an image from a hologram with a wave of wavelength different than that of the reference wave? What happens when the size of the illuminating source is increased?
2. Can you record the object wave when the object is illuminated by a beam from a laser and the reference wave is obtained from another laser?
3. A hologram is recorded by imaging the object at the recording plane where a coherent back ground wave is added to it. Can you reconstruct the image from the hologram with white light?
4. Why is a phase hologram intrinsically non-linear?
5. What must be the smallest angle between the object wave and the reference wave so that the reconstructed images are just angularly separated without any overlap?
6. Obtain an expression for the contrast of fringes in real-time hologram interferometry. How can you enhance the contrast?
7. Prove that there is no shift of the reconstructed image when a FT hologram is translated laterally.
8. Can we reconstruct a double-exposure hologram with a wave of wavelength different than that of the reference wave? What is the influence of wavelength change on the analysis of fringe pattern?
9. Calculate the angle of the wedge so that a fringe pattern of 4 mm spacing will be formed at a distance of 150 mm from the spatial filter.
10. The magnitude of small deformation can also be estimated by using a technique known as subtractive technique. Find out the sensitivity of the method.
11. Derive equation (5.6).

# 6. Speckle Phenomenon

Granular structure seen when a coherent beam falls over a diffuse object is the well-known speckle effect. It arises due to the self interference of scattered waves from the diffuser. The speckles are formed in space. They follow a certain statistics.

The speckles are usually classified under two catagories:
(a) objective type, and (b) subjective type as shown in Fig. 6.1.

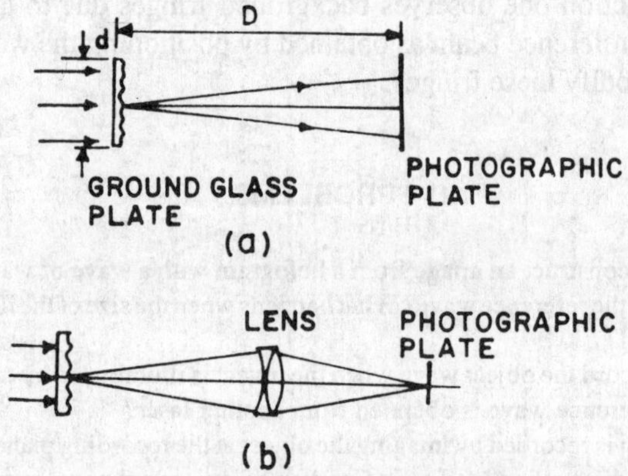


**Fig. 6.1** Recording of (a) An Objective, and (b) A Subjective Specklegram

In the case of former, a laser beam illuminates a diffuser and the speckles are formed in space. An average size may be attributed to a speckle which, in this case, is governed by the size of the diffuser being illuminated by the beam. It is given by $(\lambda/d)D$, where $d$ is the diameter of the illuminated diffuser, and $D$ is the distance between the diffuser and the observation plane. For subjective speckles, a lens is used for imaging the object at the observation plane. The average speckle size depends on the $F$ number of the lens and hence can be varied by varying the aperture of the lens.

In a situation where the object undergoes a bodily displacement, objective speckle pattern can be used for the displacement measurement. However, if the object is deformed so that every point on the surface undergoes a different displacement, speckles in the image plane are recorded. Therefore, the correspondence between the object and image points is maintained. Below we describe experiments using both objective and subjective speckles.

**Experiment 6.1:** To measure displacement given to a diffuse object.

**Equipments:** A He-Ne laser, a diffuser mounted on a translation stage, a holographic plate in the plate holder, camera lens with shutter.

**Procedure:** The schematic of the setup is shown in Fig. 6.2. An unexpanded beam of laser illuminates the diffuser. The object can be diffuse reflecting or transmitting: in this case it is a ground glass plate mounted on a translation stage and is transilluminated. The experiment can be done with both objective and subjective speckle patterns. We, however, use subjective speckle pattern and hence image the object on the recording plane, and record the speckle pattern. Now the diffuser is translated by an amount $u$ (unknown), and another exposure is made on the same photographic plate.

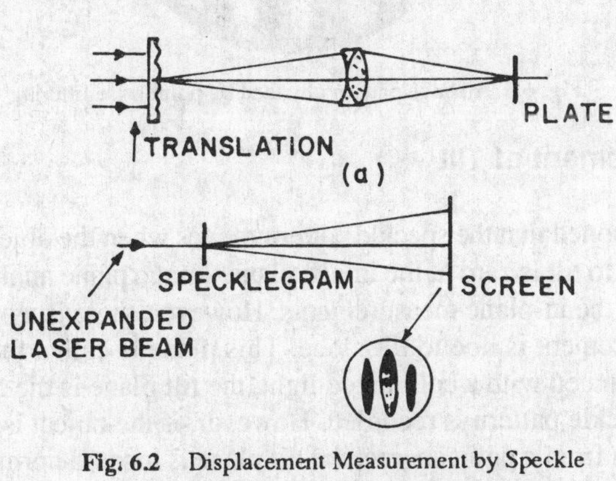


Fig. 6.2 Displacement Measurement by Speckle Photography (a) Recording, and (b) Scanning of Specklegram

Due to the translation of the diffuser, the new speckle pattern is translated with respect to the earlier one by an amount $Mu$ where $M$ is the magnification of the imaging system. In other words, the photographic plate has recorded two identical but displaced speckle patterns. The plate after development will be called specklegram.

The specklegram is illuminated with a narrow laser beam in order to obtain the value of displacement. At an observation plane distant $D$ from the specklegram, Young's fringes are observed. A typical photograph of the Young's fringes is shown in Fig. 6.3. Let the spacing of the fringes be $\bar{x}$. The spacing $\bar{x}$ is related to the displacement of speckle pattern $u$ and hence the object displacement through

$$\bar{x} = \frac{D\lambda}{Mu} \tag{6.1}$$

From this relation $u$ can be calculated provided $M$ is known. The method is known as point-wise filtering method and is also applicable to the study of specklegrams recorded without the lens. It may also be noted that the fringes are always orthogonal to the direction of displacement. As an example if a plane diffuse disc is given an in-plane rotation about its centre, the fringes will always run radially but their spacing will vary as the different regions of the image specklegram are interrogated by a narrow laser beam. Therefore, one measures both the magnitude and direction of displacement. Its sign is, however, ambiguous.

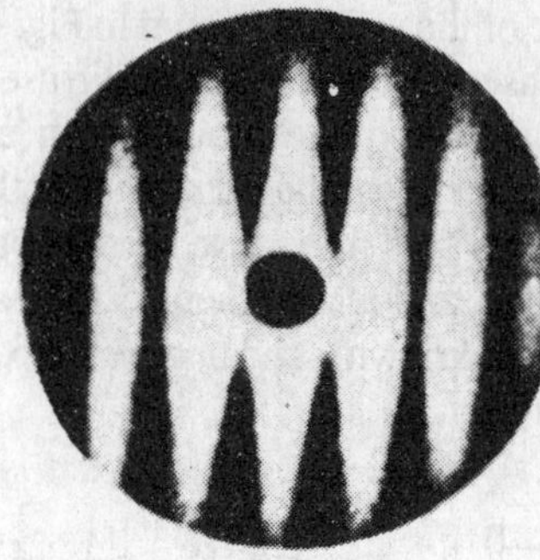

**Fig. 6.3** A fringe pattern obtained by point-wise filtering

## 6.1 Measurement of Tilt

It may be mentioned that the speckle pattern moves when the object is tilted but the movement due to tilt is zero at the image plane. Image plane analysis is, therefore, limited only to the in-plane measurements. However, there is a plane at which the speckle displacement is due to tilt alone. This plane is called the tilt plane. If an object is illuminated with a collimated light, the tilt plane is the focal plane of the lens where speckle pattern is recorded. However, if the object is illuminated by a divergent beam from a point source, the tilt plane is located normal to the axis at a point where the source point is imaged as shown in Fig. 6.4 (b).

A double exposure specklegram with tilt given to the object in between the exposures is recorded at this plane when the illumination is by a divergent beam. The information is extracted by point-wise filtering.

**Experiment 6.2:** To measure the tilt given to a diffuse object.

**Equipments:** A He-Ne laser, a diffuse object on a tilting mount, a photographic plate on a mount, a mirror, camera lens with shutter.

**Procedure:** Illuminate the object with an expanded collimated beam. For this a beam expander is setup. The diffuse object is mounted on a tilting stage and placed in the collimated beam. A camera lens is, however, used as imaging lens but the photographic plate is placed at the focal plane. In this particular case, a bright spot along with a halo is formed at the focal plane of the lens. This bright spot is due to the undiffracted beam by the object.

Having placed the photographic plate at the focal plane, a record of the speckle pattern is made. The object is now tilted. The tilt of the object will displace the speckle pattern by an amount $f\alpha$ (1+cos θ), where $\alpha$ is the tilt angle. The displaced speckle pattern is now recorded on the same photographic plate. The specklegram, therefore, contains two identical but displaced speckle patterns.

The specklegram can now be interrogated with a narrow laser beam. At a distance $D$ from the specklegram are observed Young's fringes in the diffraction halo as shown in Fig. 6.4(c). The spacing of Young's fringes $x$ is given by

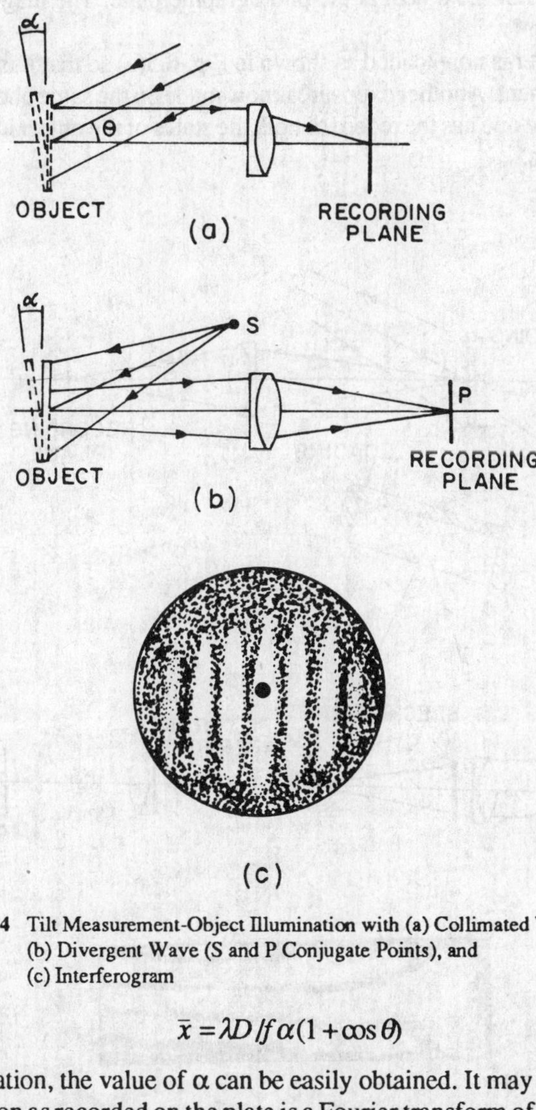


**Fig. 6.4** Tilt Measurement-Object Illumination with (a) Collimated Wave, (b) Divergent Wave (S and P Conjugate Points), and (c) Interferogram

$$\bar{x} = \lambda D / f\alpha(1+\cos\theta) \tag{6.2}$$

From this equation, the value of α can be easily obtained. It may be noted that the field distribution as recorded on the plate is a Fourier transform of the field existing on the object plane.

Similar to the specklegram of bodily displacement of the object, the tilt specklegram also gives the same information irrespective of the point of interrogation by the beam. The information about the magnitude and direction of the tilt is obtained but the sign ambiguity still remains.

**Experiment 6.3:** Full field displacement pattern of an object (a cantilever) with speckle photography.

**Equipments:** A He-Ne laser, a cantilever in its loading frame, an imaging lens, photographic plate, etc.

**Procedure:** The experimental arrangement is shown in Fig. 6.5(a). The object is illuminated with a divergent laser beam as to fill it completely. An imaging lens makes an image of the object at the photographic plate. The magnification of the system may be $M$.

The cantilever is now loaded as shown in Fig. 6.5(a) so that it is subjected to in-plane displacement. Another exposure is now made on the same photographic plate. On development one has the record of both the states of the object in the form of two speckle patterns.

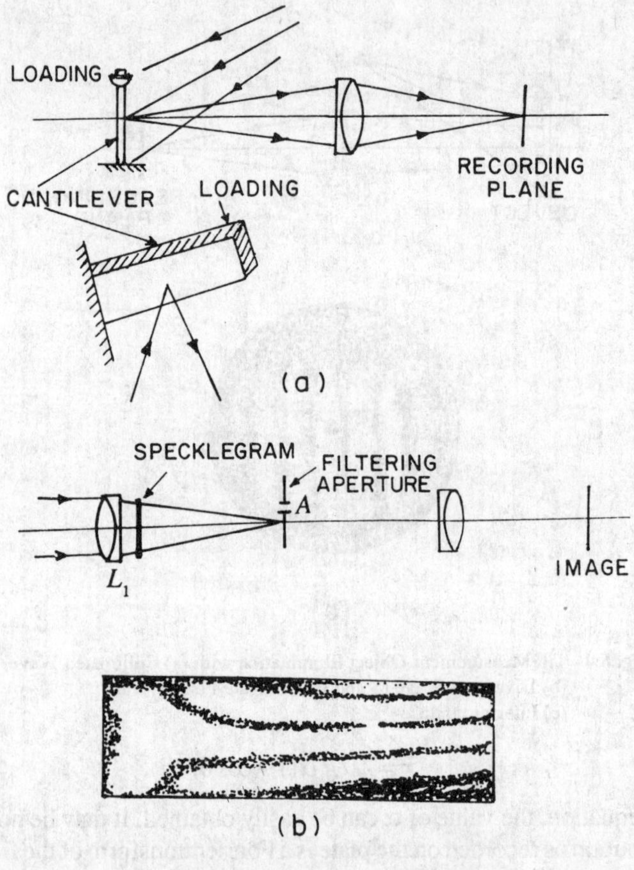


**Fig. 6.5** (a) Displacement Measurement—Cantilever as an Object and (b) Filtering Arrangement and *u* Family of Displacement Fringes

In order to obtain whole field information, a filtering setup as shown in Fig. 6.5(b) is used. The specklegram is placed either in the collimated beam infront of the lens or in the convergent beam. The lens $L_1$ displays the Fourier transform of the specklegram in its focal plane. An aperture, $A$, is used at this plane to filter the information. Another lens takes Fourier transform and the image of the object is formed at its back focal plane. This image is due to the diffracted light transmitted through the aperture and has a fringe pattern superposed on it. If the aperture is along the $x$-axis, $u$ family of displacement pattern is obtained as shown in Fig. 6.5(b). On the other hand, if the aperture is positioned along the *y*-axis, $v$ family of displacement curves is obtained. The sensitivity of the method depends directly on the displacement of *A* from the optic axis of the setup.

**Experiment 6.4:** To obtain slope contours of a diffuse object with speckle shear interferometry.

**Equipments:** A He-Ne laser, a diffuse object, a shearing arrangement and a photographic plate.

**Procedure:** The object is a diaphragm which can be loaded by a concentrated load [Fig.6.6 (a)]. This is constructed from a disc of 60 mm dia and 0.5 mm thick sheet of phosphor bronze. The disc is rigidly fixed at the periphery and loaded by translating a screw mounted at the rear plate in the center. The screw carries a ball at the tip, and its motion displaces the diaphragm at the center. There are a number of shearing

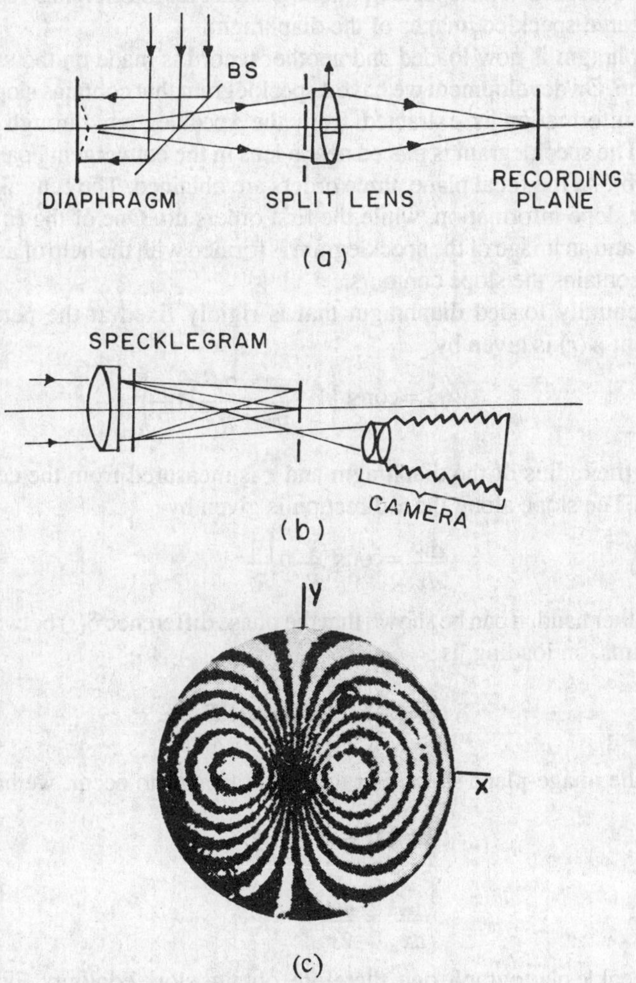


Fig. 6.6 (a) Recording, (b) Filtering arrangement, and (c) Interferogram depicting Partial Slope

arrangements in vogue. A simple but powerful arrangement can be obtained by splitting an achromat into two equal halves; one of the halves is mounted on a $x$-$y$ translation stage to translate it in its own plane. A plate having apertures of 5 mm diameter is placed in front of the lens such that each aperture is in front of the lens halves. When the two halves are so positioned that the lens act as a single full lens, only one image of the object is formed. On displacing one half relative to the other, the lens halves act as two independent lenses and form two slightly displaced (sheared) images. The image shear is $(1+M)\,x_{L_0}$ where $M$ is the magnification and $x_{L_0}$ is the displacement of lens half from complete lens position. On the object the shear is $((1+M)/M)\,x_{L_0}$ . The shear can therefore be adjusted by varying either $M$ or $x_{L_0}$. A shear of about 1 to 2% is given with the help of the micropositioner. The shear can be monitored by observing the image. The diaphragm is normally illuminated with a collimated beam. A speckle pattern in the image plane of the split lens is now recorded. This speckle pattern is infact an interference record of two slightly sheared speckled images of the diaphragm.

The diaphragm is now loaded and another record is made on the same photographic plate. On development we have a specklegram that contains slope information. This information is extracted from the specklegram through a filtering operation. The specklegram is placed near a lens in the convergent beam as shown in Fig. 6.6(b). At the focal plane, three orders are obtained. The central order does not contain slope information, while the first orders do. One of the first orders is filtered out and an image of the specklegram is formed with the help of another lens: the image contains the slope contours.

For a centrally loaded diaphragm that is rigidly fixed at the periphery, the displacement $w(r)$ is given by

$$w(r) = \text{const}\left(1 - \frac{r^2}{R^2} + \frac{2r^2}{R^2}\ln\frac{r}{R}\right) \tag{6.3}$$

where $R$ is the radius of the diaphragm and $r$ is measured from the center of the diaphragm. The slope along the $x$-direction is given by

$$\frac{dw}{dx} = \text{const}\,\frac{x}{R}\ln\frac{|x|}{R} \tag{6.4}$$

On the other hand, it can be shown that the phase difference $\delta(s)$ between the two sheared points, on loading, is

$$\delta(s) = \frac{2\pi}{\lambda}\,2\,\frac{dw}{dx}\,s = \frac{4\pi}{\lambda}\frac{dw}{dx}\,s \tag{6.5}$$

where $s$ is the image-plane shear. For the bright fringes to occur, we have

$$\frac{4\pi}{\lambda}\frac{dw}{dx}\,s = 2m\pi$$

or

$$\frac{dw}{dx} = \frac{m\lambda}{2s} \tag{6.6}$$

From the speckle photograph, one, therefore, obtains slope contours. Figure 6.6.(c) shows a photograph of $x$-slopes of a diaphragm rigidly fixed at the periphery and centrally loaded.

## 6.2 Measurement of Out-of-Plane Displacement

It has been shown earlier that the in-plane translation and the tilt of the object result in the translation of speckles on the recording plane. However, when the diffuser is axially translated, the movement of speckles on the recording plane is extremely small. Therefore, it is said that the speckle phenomenon is relatively insensitive to the measurement of the out-of-plane displacement. On the other hand, it is possible to make it sensitive by adding a reference beam, thereby recording the phase of the speckled field. A simple method is described that can be used for measuring out-of-plane displacement with holographic sensitivity.

**Experiment 6.5:** To study the deflection profile of a centrally loaded diaphragm.

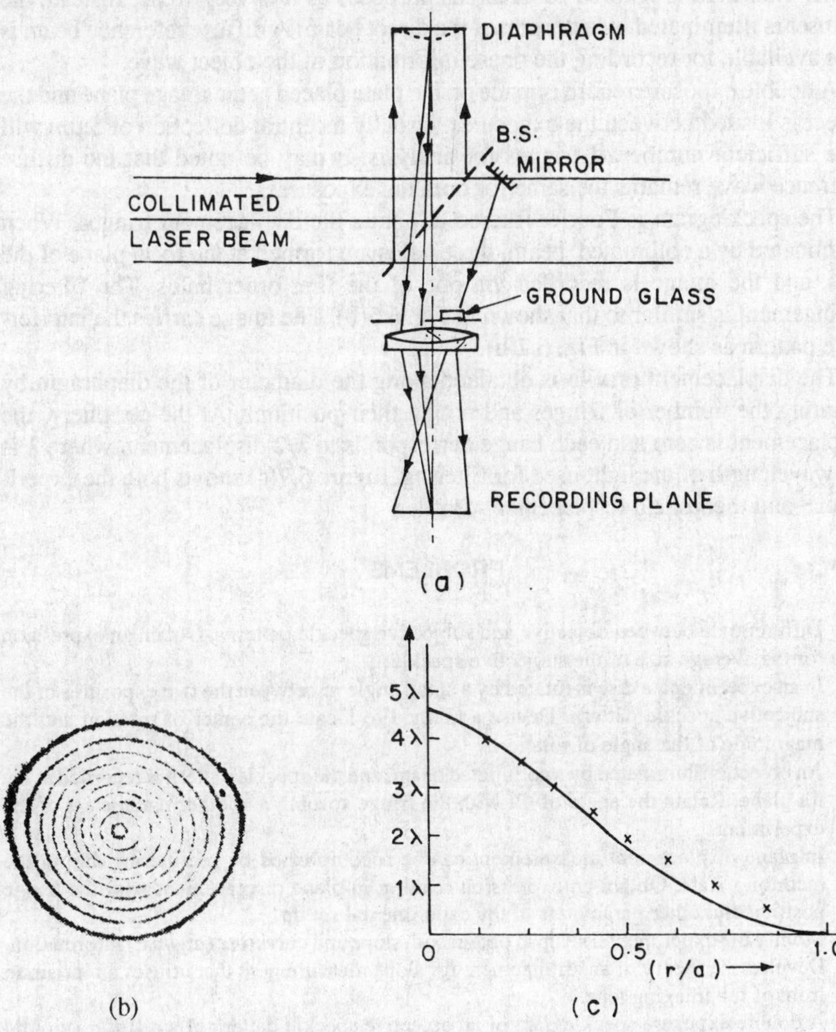


Fig. 6.7 (a) Schematic Arrangement to Measure Out-of-Plane Displacement
(b) Interferogrm
(c) Displacement Profile (x Experimental Data)

**Equipments:** A camera with a pair of apertures in front of the lens, collimator, beam splitter, a diaphragm with the loading device, He-Ne laser, holographic plate/film, Fourier filtering set up.

**Procedure:** The experimental arrangement is shown in Fig. 6.7(a). The diaphragm is identical to that described in Experiment 6.4. A collimated beam of size slightly larger than the diameter of the diaphragm is produced. This beam is directed by a beam splitter to illuminate the object (diaphragm). The camera with a pair of apertures infront of the lens is mounted as shown in Fig. 6.7(a). A ground glass plate is mounted on one of the apertures. The other aperture is used to let the scattered field from the object for imaging. An extremely weak beam from the object as it is further scattered by the ground glass plate on the other aperture also reaches the image plane. This field is ignored for analysis purposes as it is very weak. Instead, the diffuser is illuminated by a portion of the direct beam. A diffuse reference beam is thus available for recording the phase information of the object wave.

A double exposure record is made on the plate placed at the image plane and the object is loaded between the exposures. Usually a central deflection of 5 $\mu m$ will give sufficient number of fringes for analysis. It may be noted that the diffuse reference-wave remains the same for both the exposures.

The specklegram is Fourier filtered to obtain the displacement fringes. When illuminated by a collimated beam, three halos are formed at the focal plane of the lens, and the image is recorded via one of the first order halos. The filtering arrangement is similar to that shown in Fig. 6.6(b). The image carries the interference pattern as shown in Fig. 6.7(b).

The displacement profile is obtained along the diameter of the diaphragm by counting the number of fringes and noting their positions. At the periphery, the displacement is zero and each fringe corresponds to $\lambda/2$ displacement, where $\lambda$ is the wavelength of the light used for filtering. Figure 6.7(c) shows both the experimental and theoretical displacement profiles.

## PROBLEMS

1. Differentiate between objective and subjective speckle patterns. Obtain an expression for the average size of the subjective speckle.
2. In an experiment, a disc is rotated by a small angle in between the two exposures of the subjective speckle pattern. Devise a method to locate the center of rotation and the magnitude of the angle of rotation.
3. An object is illuminated by a collimated beam, and the speckle pattern is recorded at the tilt plane. Relate the angle of tilt with the fringe spacing and other parameters of the experiment.
4. In-plane displacement measurement can be accomplished by prefiltering during the recording state. Obtain an expression relating in-plane displacement with the fringe position and other parameters of the experimental set up.
5. Modify the experimental setup to obtain both slope and curvature ($d^2w/dx^2$) information.
6. Develop the theory of an arrangement for slope measurement that utilises a biprism in front of the imaging lens.
7. A double exposure specklegram of an objective speckle pattern of a diffuser (ground glass) with an axial displacement given to the diffuser between the exposures is filtered. How do we obtain the magnitude of the axial displacement from the observed fringe pattern?

# 7. Spatial Filtering

The areas like optical processing, spatial frequency filtering, holography, etc. can be grouped under the heading of coherent optics. In this chapter we shall, however, restrict to the Abbe's theory of imaging which includes some of the basic ideas of coherent optics and some simple experiments involving the manipulation of the diffraction pattern (Fourier transform) of the object to achieve desired features in the image.

It is well-known that if a transparency is kept at the front focal plane of a well corrected lens and illuminated with a collimated beam, its Fourier transform is displayed at the back focal plane. The Fourier transform of any two dimensional signal is physically available for manipulation. Let $\tau(x_1, y_1)$ be the amplitude transmittance of the transparency located at the front focal plane (Fig. 7.1). The amplitude $u_2(x_2, y_2)$ at the back focal plane is given by

$$u_2(x_2, y_2) = c\iint \tau(x_1, y_1) \exp[-2\pi i(x_1x_2+y_1y_2)/\lambda f_1]dx_1dy_1 \qquad (7.1)$$

where $f_1$ is the focal length of the lens and $c$ is a complex constant.

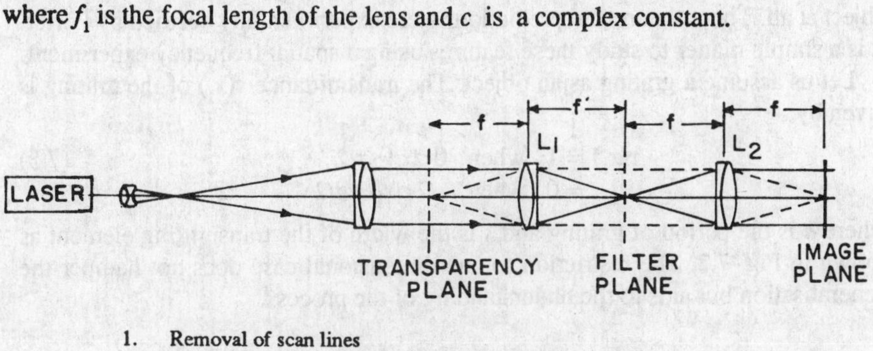


1. Removal of scan lines
   Transparency —A negative from TV screen picture
   Filter—An adjustable slit in rotatable mount
2. Removal of half tones
   Transparency—A negative of a newspaper photograph
   Filter—A pin hole of an appropriate size

**Fig. 7.1** Schematic of an Optical Data Processing Setup

Defining the spatial frequencies $\mu$ and $\nu$ as

$$\mu = \frac{x_2}{\lambda f_1} \quad \text{and} \quad \nu = \frac{y_2}{\lambda f_1} \qquad (7.2)$$

the amplitude at the back focal plane is given by

$$u_2(\mu, \nu) = c \iint \tau(x_1, y_1) \exp[-2\pi i(\mu x_1 + \nu y_1)] dx_1 dy_1 \tag{7.3}$$

Thus a Fourier transform relationship exists between

$$\tau(x_1, y_1) \quad \text{and} \quad u_2(\mu, \nu).$$

If we use one more lens of focal length $f_2$ for further Fourier transformation, i.e., the back focal plane of the first lens is coincident with the front focal plane of the second lens, the amplitude distribution $u_3(x_3, y_3)$ at its back focal plane is given by

$$u_3(x_3, y_3) = C'\tau\left(-\frac{f_2}{f_1}x_1, -\frac{f_2}{f_1}y_1\right) \tag{7.4}$$

It may be seen that $(x_1 - y_1)$ and $(x_3 - y_3)$ planes are conjugate planes. The image of the transparency is thus magnified by $(f_2/f_1)$ and is inverted.

## 7.1 Abbe's Theory of Image Formation

Abbe formulated the theory of imaging in a microscope under coherent illumination as a two step process, first involving diffraction at the object and then at the microscope objective. The object is usually kept just outside the front focal plane of the microscope objective. Therefore, the object spectrum is displayed at the back focal plane. The waves from the spectrum will propagate further and interfere to give an image of the object. If the numerical aperture of the objective is sufficiently large to accept the largest diffraction angle of the light diffracted by the object, an ideal image of the object will be formed. If the objective does not accept all the diffracted light, i.e., the diffraction at the objective takes place, some details in the image will be missing. Under certain conditions the image may not resemble the object at all. These theoretical predictions were experimentally verified by Porter. It is a simple matter to study these features using a spatial frequency experiment.

Let us assume a grating as an object. The transmittance $\tau(x_1)$ of the grating is given by

$$\begin{aligned} \tau(x_1) &= 1 \quad \text{when} \quad 0 < |x_1| \leq s/2 \\ &= 0 \quad \text{when} \quad s/2 < |x_1| \leq d/2 \end{aligned} \tag{7.5}$$

where $d$ is the period of grating and $s$ is the width of the transmitting element as shown in Fig. 7.2. The restriction to one dimensional case does not hamper the generalisation but aids to the understanding of the process.

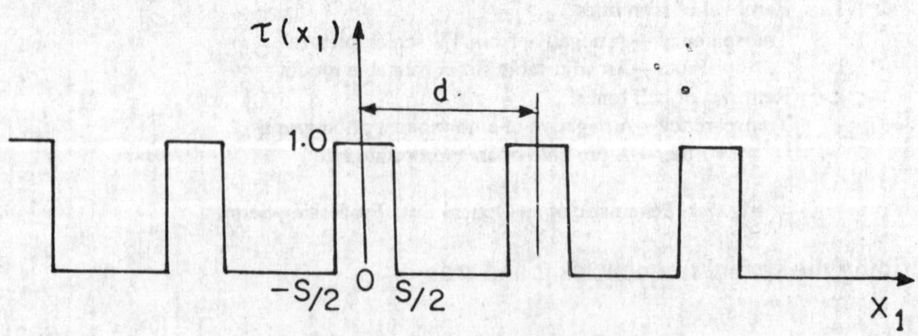


Fig. 7.2 Grating of Rectangular Profile

The transmittance $\tau(x_1)$ can be expanded in a series as:

$$(x_1) = A_0 + 2\sum_{m=1}^{\infty} A_m \cos\left(\frac{2\pi m x_1}{d}\right) \tag{7.6}$$

where $A_0 = \frac{s}{d}$ *and* $A_m = \frac{s}{d} \sin\left(\frac{2\pi m s}{d}\right)$.

Let us now consider a spatial filtering experiment as shown in Fig. 7.3. The grating is located at the front focal plane of lens $L_1$. Its Fourier transform that consists of an infinity of orders (δ-functions) centered at $x_2 = \pm m\lambda f_1/d$ is displayed as bright dots of decreasing irradiance at the back focal plane. It is, however, assumed that lens $L_1$ accepts all the diffracted beams from the grating. If the lens $L_2$ has sufficiently large aperture to accept the beams from all the diffraction orders, an image identical to $\tau(x_1)$ is formed at its back focal plane. Let us now consider some situations where some of the diffraction orders have been deliberately eliminated from the imaging process:

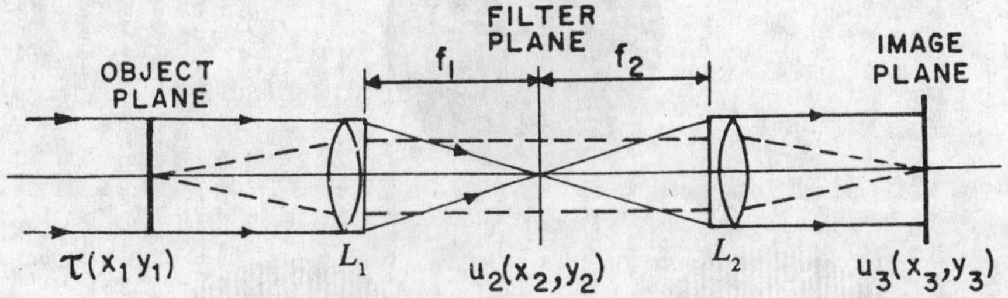


**Fig. 7.3** Imaging as Double Fourier Transformation

1. All orders but the zero order are blocked: The image plane now appears uniformly illuminated. The zero order does not carry any details of the grating but provides only a bias.
2. All higher orders except 0 and ±1 orders are blocked: The image has the same periodicity as that of the grating but a different profile. The image, instead of being of rectangular profile, is of sinusoidal profile.
3. All orders except 0 and ±2 orders are blocked: The image is of sinusoidal profile but of twice the frequency (half the periodicity) of the object grating. Thus completely false details appear in the image.

We, therefore, conclude that all the diffraction orders should contribute to the image formation for obtaining a faithful image of the object. In cases where certain orders are eliminated, some details will be necessarily missing in the image. The contribution of first order to the image formation is particularly important as it provides the correct periodicity.

If we consider a two dimensional grating as an object, its Fourier transform will consist of diagonal orders along with orders perpendicular to the grating elements, say along horizontal and vertical directions. Using a narrow slit all the orders but those along the horizontal direction can be blocked. The image will now contain a grating with vertical elements. Similarly, if the slit allows only the vertical orders, the image will be a grating with horizontal elements. By proper orientation of slit, diagonal orders can be selected for image formation. The image will now contain a grating with elements inclined with either horizontal or vertical. This is an example where completely false image is obtained.

The optical and mathematical theory outlined above gains new dimensions when its effects become visible; what was once an abstract understanding seems an experience in reality. This experience is indeed gained when some simple experiments are performed with laser light.

**Experiment 7.1:** Demonstration of Abbe's theory of image formation.

**Equipments:** A spatial filtering setup (a beam expander, two lenses of about 500 mm focal length), transparencies ( a linear grating, a wire mesh), an adjustable slit on the mount and a screen.

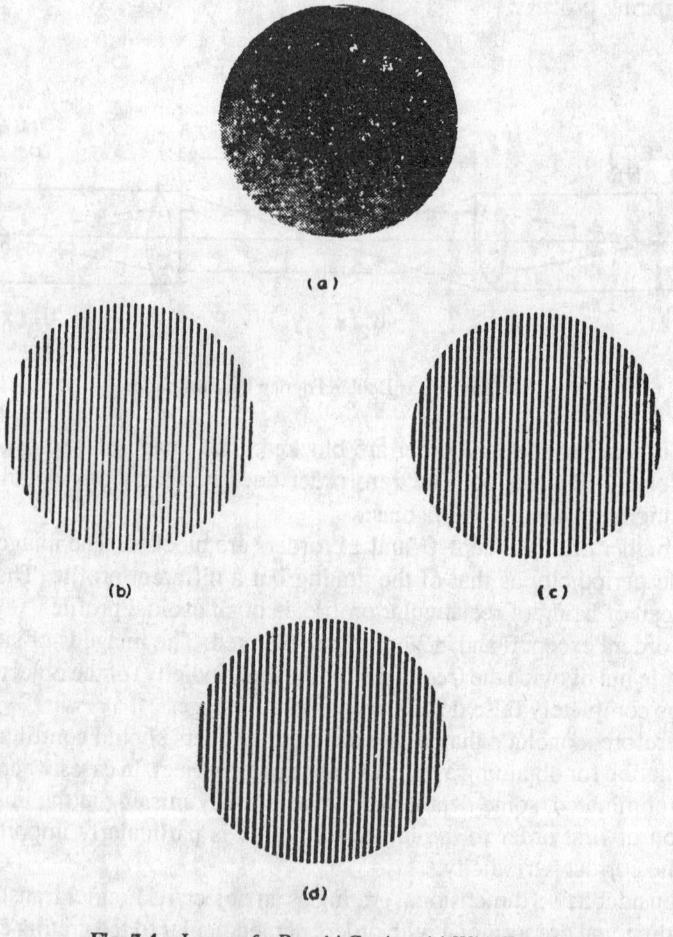


Fig. 7.4 Image of a Ronchi Grating: (a) With Zero Order; (b) With Zero and the First Orders; (c) With Zero and ±3-Orders; and (d) With All Orders

**Procedure:** Figure 7.1 illustrates an arrangement of a spatial filtering setup. The laser beam is expanded and collimated using a beam expander. A suitable expansion of the beam is done depending on the power of the laser available. The transparency (linear grating) is mounted on the front focal plane of the lens $L_1$. Its spectrum is displayed at its back focal plane where the adjustable slit is positioned. If the grating elements are vertical, its spectrum will lie in horizontal line. A slit with its jaws vertical is now placed at this plane. Lens $L_2$ is positioned such that its front focal plane is the slit plane. A screen is placed at its back focal plane. The spatial filtering experiment requires a fairly long optical bench (>3 meters long).

An illustrative experiment can be performed by a linear grating (4 l/mm) as a transparency and a variable slit as spatial filter. The spectrum of the grating will contain a large number of dots; the central dot (zero order) being the brightest. The slit is positioned and adjusted such that it allows only the zero order. Only uniform illumination will be observed at the screen. If the slit is opened as to allow 0 and ±1 orders for image formation, the image will be a sinusoidal grating of correct periodicity.

Figure 7.4 shows the photographs of the images wherein (a) only zero order, (b) zero order and first orders, (c) zero order and third orders, and (d) all the diffraction orders are allowed to contribute to the image formation.

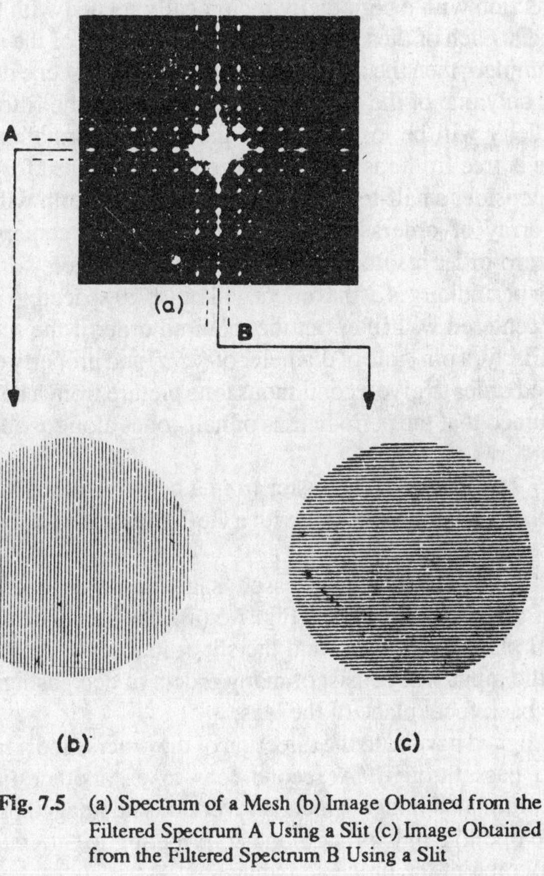


Fig. 7.5 (a) Spectrum of a Mesh (b) Image Obtained from the Filtered Spectrum A Using a Slit (c) Image Obtained from the Filtered Spectrum B Using a Slit

Another interesting experiment can be performed with a wire mesh (two dimensional grating) as a transparency. The spectrum will contain prominent horizontal and vertical orders along with the cross diagonal orders as shown in Fig. 7.5(a). If the slit allows either vertical or horizontal orders, an image having either horizontal or vertical grating elements will be formed. Fig. 7.5(b) and (c) show the images of the wire mesh formed with vertical and horizontal orders respectively.

## 7.2 Low-Pass Filtering

A popular application of low-pass filtering is to remove rastor from a television type picture. A two-dimensional equivalent of this application is the removal of half-tone to produce a continuous tone image. The filtered images show scene details that are not observable in the half-tone pictures. The low-pass filtering is done using a filter that permits transfer of only low spatial frequency contents for image formation.

The well known examples of low pass filters are a pin-hole and a variable slit.

Let us first understand the physical process of rastor removal. The scene which is continuous has been periodically sampled with a rastor period. The Fourier transform of the input (sampled scene) consists of a distribution which is periodic along one direction with a periodicity reciprocally related with the rastor periodicity. Centered at each of these locations is the transform of the scene. If the scene is correctly sampled, then the individual transform of the scene do not overlap with each other. If only one of the transform is permitted by the filter, the information about periodicity will be lost, and only the scene information is retained. The filtered image is free from rastor. Usually zero order is used for image formation.

When we consider a half-tone input, its Fourier transform will consist of a two-dimensional array of orders with the scene transform centered at each order. Selection of zero-order results in a continuous tone image.

If the rastor periodicity is $d$, the orders will be $(\lambda f/d)$ spaced. A slit of $(\lambda f/d)$ width and properly centered will filter out the required order if the scene was correctly sampled. Similarly, a pin-hole of diameter of $(\lambda f/d)$ and properly centered will filter out the required order to give a continuous tone picture from a half-tone input. It is, however, assumed that the periodicities of half-tones along $x$ and $y$ are same, and equal to $d$.

**Experiment 7.2:** To remove the rastor from a negative of a TV picture.

**Equipments:** A coherent processor with a He-Ne laser, a variable width slit, and a screen.

**Procedure:** The input to the processor is a transparency of a TV picture; a photograph of the same is shown in Fig. 7.6 (a). The transparency is positioned at the front-focal plane of the lens, and the slit at its back focal plane. The Fourier transform of the input will consist of many orders of decreasing irradiances when viewed at the back focal plane of the lens.

The slit is aligned normal to the direction of the orders, and adjusted to allow the zero order to pass through. A second lens takes another Fourier transform, producing a continuous image which is inverted. The image appears of relatively low irradiance due to single order alone contributing to the image. Figure 7.6(b) shows a photograph of the processed image.

(a) (b)

**Fig. 7.6** Rastor Removal: (a) Original Picture, and (b) Image Obtained by Filtering Zero Order

## 7.3 Synthesis of Vander Lugt Filter and Character Recognition

For matched filtering, character recognition and deblurring problems, etc. a complex filter is required. The complex filter alters both the amplitude and phase of the spectrum. For matched filtering a filter matched to the input $\tau(x_1, y_1)$ is to be synthesised. The transfer function of the filter should be

$$H(\mu, \nu) = T^*(\mu, \nu) \tag{7.7}$$

where $T^*(\mu, \nu) = F[\tau(x_1, y_1)]$, and $F$ stands for Fourier transform operation.

The filter that has transfer function $T^*(\mu, \nu)$ is synthesised following the procedure described below:

**Experiment 7.3:** To synthesise Vander Lugt filter.

**Equipments:** A coherent processor with He-Ne laser.

**Procedure:** The processor is set up, and the input transparency $\tau(x_1, y_1)$ is located at the front focal plane of the lens. The Fourier transform $T(\mu, \nu)$ of the input is formed at the back focal plane. At this plane is added a plane wave to the Fourier transform. Figure 7.7(a) shows the schematic diagram of the setup. The plane wave makes an angle $\theta$ with the optic axis. A photographic plate placed at the back focal plane records the interference between the plane wave and the Fourier transform. The exposure recorded is given by

$$E = \left|\left[e^{2\pi i \mu_0 x} + T(\mu, \nu)\right]\right|^2 t, \tag{7.8}$$

where $\mu_0 = \frac{\sin\theta}{\lambda}$ (and $\mu = x/\lambda f$, $\nu = y/\lambda f$ and $t$ is the exposure time.

Assuming linear recording, the amplitude transmittance of the processed photographic plate is given by

$$\hat{T}(x, y) = \hat{t}_0 - \beta E$$

$$= \hat{t}_0' - \beta t[|T(\mu, \nu)|^2 + T(\mu, \nu)\, e^{2\pi i \mu_0 x} + T^*(\mu, \nu)\, e^{2\pi i \mu_0 x})] \tag{7.9}$$

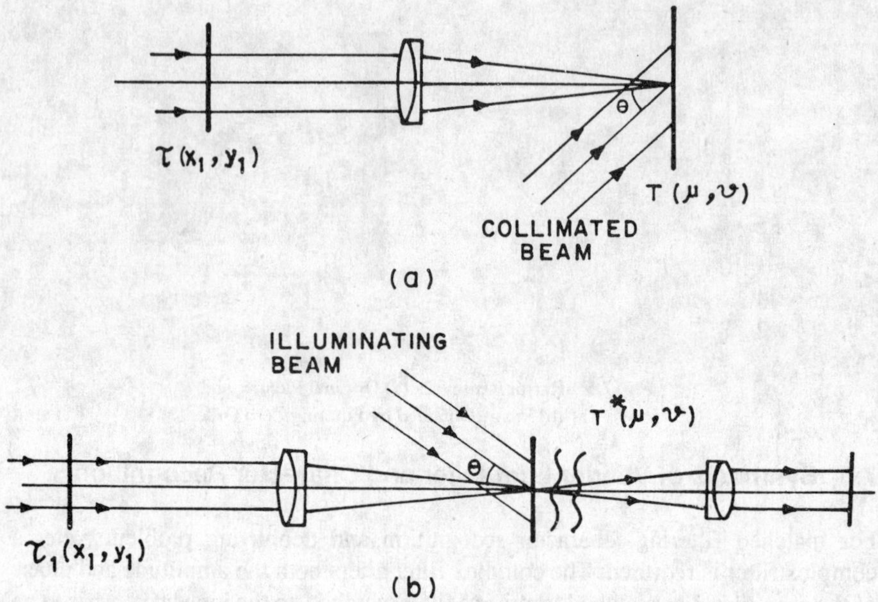


Fig. 7.7 Fabrication of (a) Vander Lugt Filter, and (b) Its Use

If transparency $\hat{\tau}(x, y)$, now called a filter, is positioned at the back focal plane, and illuminated with a plane wave making an angle $(-\theta)$ with the axis, a field proportional to $T^*(\mu, \nu)$ will be released along the optic axis. This is, therefore, the right configuration for matched filtering [Fig. 7.7 (b)].

If the input to the processor contains some characters for which the filter has been synthesised, the output will exhibit peaks wherever the characters are present. As an example, the input may be a photograph of all the numbers beginning 1 to 100. The filter is synthesised for input character say of 5. The output will exhibit prominent spots at 20 locations where the character 5 is present.

If the Fourier transform of $\tau(x, y)$ is recorded on the photographic plate, i.e, $|T(\mu, \nu)|^2$ is recorded. The amplitude transmittance of the transparency will be where

$$\tau(\mu, \nu) = [|T(\mu, \nu)|^2]^{(-\gamma/2)}, \tag{7.10}$$

$\gamma$ is the gamma of the emulsion. If the processing is done such that $\gamma = -1$, then

$$\tau(\mu, \nu) = |T(\mu, \nu)| \tag{7.11}$$

Such a filter, when used in an optical processor will give the auto-correlation of the input function.

## 7.4 Theta Modulation

Theta modulation provides a very powerful technique for analog to digital conversion. In a picture, areas having the same amplitude transmittance can be modulated with gratings of same pitch and orientation, and hence can be filtered out. We describe, hence, extremely simple experiment that demonstrates the principles of $\theta$-modulation. The input transparency can be easily prepared. In this experiment two letters $R$ and $H$ are modulated by a Ronchi grating. The orientations of the Ronchi grating are different for the two letters. At the frequency plane diffraction patterns belonging to the gratings (being always orthogonal to the grating elements) are displayed. If the object scene is properly sampled, each order has the scene information. A pin-hole is used to filter one of the orders other than the zero order.

An interesting alternative to $\theta$-modulation is to keep the orientation of the gratings same but vary only their frequency. The appropriate orders can be used for image formation. This technique may be called frequency modulation. This also provides similar capabilities.

In practice both these techniques of $\theta$-modulation and frequency modulation are combined to provide for larger number of grey levels.

**Experiment 7.4:** Filtering using $\theta$-modulati n.

**Equipments:** A spatial filtering arrangement, an input transparency, a pin-hole in $x$-$y$ mount, ground glass plate or a camera.

**Procedure:** The spatial filtering arrangement is setup as described earlier. The input, which is a combination of letters $R$ and $H$ modulated by the gratings, is

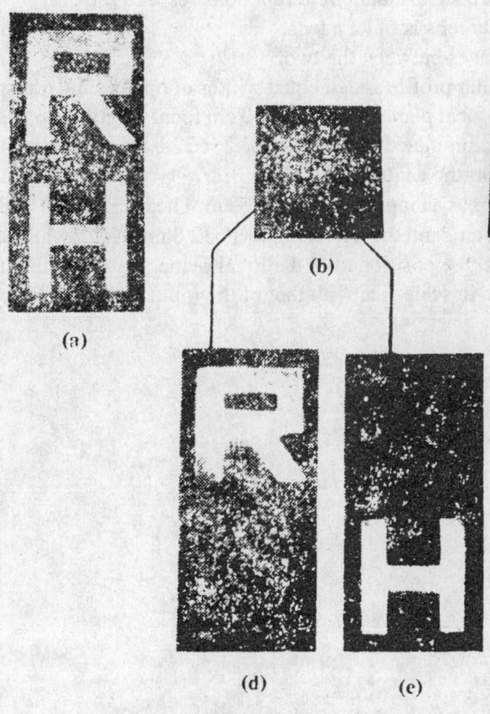

**Fig. 7.8** Theta Modulation (a) An Input Transparency: $R$ Modulated by Vertical and $H$ by Horizontal Lines, (b) Its Fourier Transform, (c) Recording Away from the Fourier Plane, (d) Image from First order and (e) Image from First-Order

placed at the input plane. Figure 7.8(a) gives the enlarged photograph of the input. The spectrum of the input is displayed at the frequency plane, where the pin-hole is mounted. The appearance of the spectrum is shown in Fig. 7.8(b). Since the letters are modulated with gratings of the same pitch but orientation of 90° apart, the spectrum consists of two grating patterns. The zero order carries informations about both the letters, while the horizontal orders contain information about letter *R* and vertical orders about letter *H*. If the recording is made at a plane a little distance away from the Fourier plane a pattern as shown in Fig. 7.8(c) is obtained which validates the above statement. One of the first orders from the horizontal row is filtered out by a pin-hole, and the filtered image is as shown in Fig. 7.8(d). Only letter *R* is imaged, and letter *H* is completely blocked. Similarly, if an order from the vertical column is used for image formation, only letter *H* will be imaged as shown in Fig. 7.8(e).

## PROBLEMS

1. Show that a lens introduces a phase of $\exp[\pm i\pi(x^2+y^2)/\lambda f]$ where $f$ is its focal length.
2. Prove that the sinusoidal grating will give only 0 and ± 1 orders.
3. The two diffracting screens are characterised by the following transmittance functions:
   3.1 $\tau(r)=[0.5+0.5 \text{ sgn } (\cos ar^2)] \text{ circ } (r/R)$
   3.2 $\tau(r)=[0.5+0.5 \cos ar^2] \text{ circ } (r/R)$
   where sgn and circ are signus and circle functions respectively.
   Show that both the screens act like a lens.
   Point out the differences between the two.
4. A grating of rectangular profile and of equal widths of opaque and transparent portions is placed at the front focal plane of a lens of 10 cm focal length. The grating frequency is 5.1/mm, and it is illuminated by the light of $\lambda$=632.8 nm. Calculate the separations of various orders from the central order.
5. A coherent processor has an input aperture of 3 cm. The focal length of the first Fourier Transform lens is 15 cm, and the wavelength is 632.8 nm. With what accuracy must a frequency-plane mask be positioned in the focal plane, assuming that the mask has a structure comparable in scale size with that of the input spectrum ?

# 8. Laser Doppler Anemometry

Laser anemometer enables the measurement of instantaneous velocity of a gas or liquid flowing in a glass walled channel. This has the following unique features:

(i) non-contact measurement
(ii) excellent spatial resolution
(ii) very fast response to the fluctuating velocity fields
(iv) no transfer function involved: the output is linearly proportional to the velocity, and
(v) measurement possibilities in both gaseous and liquid flows.

This, however, is restricted to bubbly flows; the flows that carry suspensions to scatter light. The particle density of suspensions should not be less than $10^{10}$ particles/mm$^3$. The suspension size in gases ranges from 1 to 5 μm, and in water from 2 to 10 μm. The suspended particles should follow the flow faithfully.

The theory and operation of the Laser Doppler Anemometer (LDA) is based on the following:

The frequency of radiation scattered by a particle moving relative to a radiating source is changed by an amount that depends on the velocity and the scattering geometry. Consider a laser beam of circular frequency $\omega_0$ propagating along the unit vector $\bar{c}_1$. If the light scattered along the unit vector $\bar{c}_2$ by a scatterer moving with a velocity $\bar{v}$ is examined, its circular frequency $\omega_s$ is given by

$$\omega_s = \omega_0 + n_0 \bar{v} \cdot (\bar{k}_s - \bar{k}_i)$$

where $n_0$ is the refractive index of the medium, and $\bar{k}_i$ $(=(2\pi/\lambda_0)\ \bar{c}_1)$ and $\bar{k}_s$ $(=(2\pi/\lambda_0)\ \bar{c}_2)$ are the propagation vectors of the incident and scattered waves respectively. The Doppler frequency $\Delta v_D$ is given by

$$\Delta v_D = (\omega_s - \omega_0)/2\pi$$

$$= \frac{2n_0 v}{\lambda_0} \sin(\theta/2) \sin\beta$$

where the angles $\theta$ and $\beta$ are shown in Fig. 8.1. If $\beta = (\pi/2)$, then the velocity $v$ is given by

$$v = \Delta v_D \frac{\lambda_0}{n_0} \frac{1}{2\sin(\theta/2)}$$

The velocity $v$ is linearly related to the Doppler frequency. This is the basic formula for the Laser Doppler Anemometry.

## 8.1 LDA Configurations

There are two distinct approaches in vogue to use the LDA. These are

(i) reference beam mode, and

(ii) interference fringe mode.

In the reference beam mode, the laser beam is split into two beams which are directed at the point of measurement in the field at an angle $\theta$. The light scattered in the direction is picked up and photo-mixed in the photo-multiplier tube (PMT) with the reference beam propagating in the same direction as shown in Fig. 8.2(a). The PMT yields a signal which is processed to obtain Doppler frequency. The reference beam need not traverse through the same medium, but can be added to the scattered beam at PMT surface. Usually the reference beam is

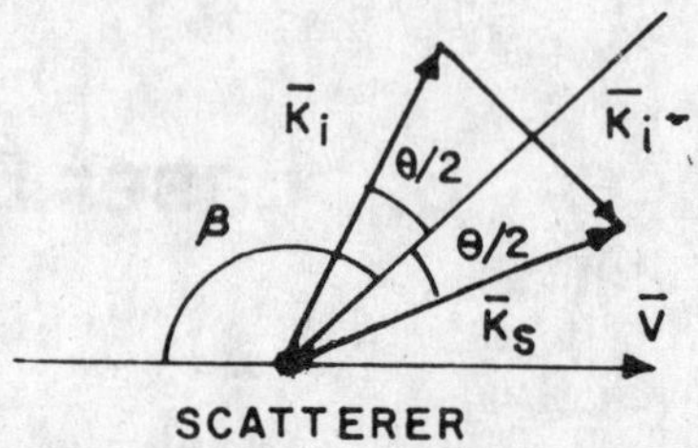


**Fig. 8.1** Geometry for Scattering

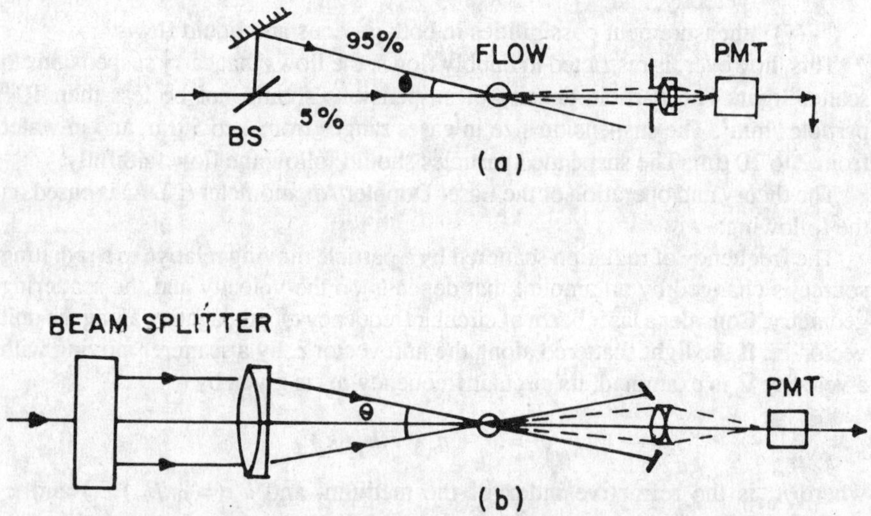


**Fig. 8.2** (a) Reference Mode Geometry and (b) Fringe Mode Geometry

considerably weaker (say 5% of the incident beam) than the other beam, so that the scattered beam is relatively stronger and a good heterodyne signal from PMT is obtained. This mode of operation can be used with advantage when the suspension density is fairly high. Further the alignment tolerance required for heterodyne process is not so critical, and hence it is relatively easy to use.

The working principle of the interference fringe mode gives a better insight into the appearance of Doppler signal. The schematic of the fringe mode anemometer is shown in Fig. 8.2(b). The beam from the laser is symmetrically split by a beam splitter, and then focussed in the flow by a lens $L_1$. In the region of intersection of these two beams, Young's interference fringes are formed with a spacing $\bar{x}$ where (Fig. 8.3)

$$\bar{x} = \frac{\lambda f}{s} = \frac{\lambda_0}{2n_0 \sin(\theta/2)}$$

where $s$ is the separation between the beams sand $f$ is the focal length of the lens $L_1$. The fringes are parallel to the bisector of angle between the two beams. As a particle moves across this fringe pattern, it passes through planes of maximum and

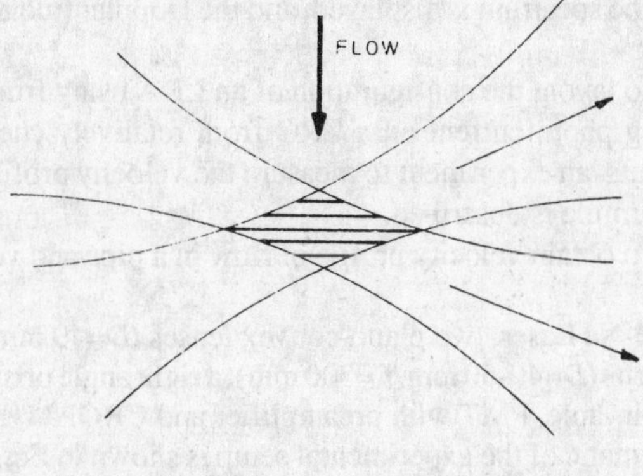


**Fig. 8.3** Interference fringes in sample volume

minimum irradiances. When it is at the bright fringe (plane of maximum irradiance) it scatters more light. Therefore, as the particle traverses the interference field normal to the fringes, it scatters light which generates a periodic signal with a frequency

$$2\sin(\theta/2)\,\frac{n_0}{\lambda_0}\,v$$

The scattered light is collected by another lens in the pick-up unit. The sample volume (interference region) is imaged on a pin-hole in front of the detector. This is the most critical alignment to get a good Doppler signal. A filter for the laser wavelength is placed behind the pin-hole and in front of the PMT so that the anemometer can be run under normal lighting conditions. The output of the PMT when displayed over CRO appears as shown in Fig. 8.4. The velocity signal rides over a strong dc background.

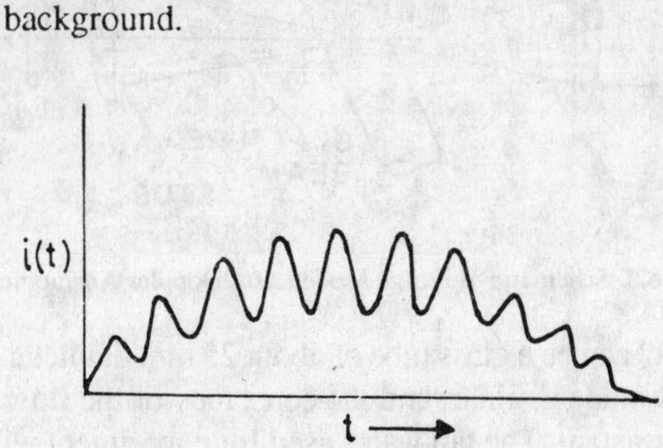


**Fig. 8.4** Photocurrent Output from PMT

Using a storage oscilloscope, the output of PMT can be displayed, and the period between two peaks can be calculated. This is used to calculate the velocity. However, this is of limited use. Indeed there are two approaches to process the LDA signal. In time domain approach, the photo-current (output of PMT) is fed to an auto-correlator. It is known that the Fourier transform of an auto-correlation function is the power spectrum. Thus the output of the auto-correlator is digitised, and used as an input to obtain FT on a digital computer. This gives both the peak (Doppler frequency) and width of the spectrum. Alternately a Spectrum Analyser can be used where the spectrum is displayed, and the Doppler frequency is directly read off.

Since it is easy to layout the configuration of an LDA using fringe mode to the extent of displaying photo current on a CRO from relatively cheap and readily available components, an experiment to measure the velocity profile in a pipe and verify Poiseuille formula is described.

**Experiment 8.1:** To obtain velocity profile of flow in a pipe and verify Poiseuille formula.

**Equipments:** A He-Ne Laser, two plano-convex lenses ($D$=40 mm, $f$=200 mm), one plano-convex lens ($D$=40-50 mm, $f$=300 mm), a right angle prism, a cube beam splitter, a filter, a pin-hole, PMT with preamplifier and CRO.

**Procedure:** A schematic of the experimental setup is shown in Fig. 8.5. A laser of 2 mW to 5 mW output and very low amplitude variations is ideally suited for the purpose. The beam is split into two beams by the cube beam splitter: one beam proceeds straight while the other is folded to run parallel by the right angle prism. The separation between the beams is kept between 30 and 35 mm. The beams are incident on the plano-convex lens assembly: both the plano-convex lenses are assembled such that they have a common focus, and can be translated as a unit so that the common focus traverses a certain distance in the flow pipe. The flow pipe is kept normally to the angle bisector of the beams. The lens $L_3$ is used to image the sample volume (region of beams intersection) at the pin-hole. The location of sample volume is varied inside the pipe by traversing the lens assembly.

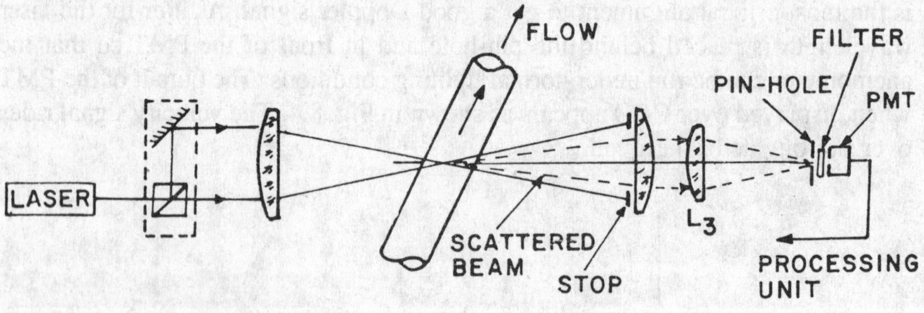


**Fig. 8.5** Schematic of Fringe Mode Laser Doppler Anemometer

The flow channel can be a glass tube of about 25 mm diameter, and of sufficient length. The flow is made laminar, and the constancy of the flow is maintained by keeping the head constant. The tap water used for experiment will not require any seeding as there is already a sufficiently large particle density.

The Doppler frequency is usually in audio-range, and often a headphone is used for hearing the Doppler frequency, and then maximising the Doppler signal by properly superposing the two beams with the help of right angle prism.

When the Doppler signal is optimum, it can be displayed on CRO to obtain the time between two peaks.

The measurements are made at a number of positions of the sample volume in the channel, and the corresponding flow velocities are calculated. The location of sample volume is changed by moving the plano-convex lens assembly along the beams. The traverse of this assembly can be read off from a scale mounted on the bench. Therefore, a plot between velocity and the position of the sample volume can be drawn, and compared with that obtained from theory.

The experimental setup excluding laser, water tanks and CRO, is to be mounted on a vibration isolated table. The wall of transparent tube does not change the sample volume, but merely displaces it, and hence there is no influence of windows.

## PROBLEMS

1. Calculate the flow of water ($n$=1.33) in m/sec., when a beam from a He-Ne laser ($\lambda$ = 632 nm) scattered at an angle of 2.7° beats with a reference beam to give a Doppler frequency of 10 MHz.
2. The irradiance distribution of a beam at the lens surface is expressed as

$$I(r) = I_0 \exp(-r^2/2\sigma^2)$$

   where $4\sigma$ is the beam waist. Show that the beam waist $4\sigma'$ at the focal plane of the lens of focal length $f$ is given by

$$4\sigma' = \frac{\lambda f}{\pi n_0 \sigma}$$

3. A beam of 5 mm diameter is split into two beams which are separated by 30 mm. The beams are brought to focus by a lens of 100 mm focal length. Calculate (i) the beam waist size, and hence the sample volume at the focal plane, and (ii) the flow velocity normal to the fringes when a signal at 150 KHz is observed.
4. Sketch a schematic for studying velocity fields in the backward scattering geometry from the suspensions.

# Appendix A

# Alignment of Laser

Commercial He-Ne lasers are available with either internal mirrors or external mirrors laser heads. The former gives unpolarised output of a few milliwatt (usually not exceeding 5 mW) and are factory aligned and sealed. There is no provision of any alignment during usage. The external mirrors laser heads have laser tubes that are enclosed by Brewster windows, and a pair of mirrors on adjustable mounts at either end of the tube that form the resonator. The mirrors are factory aligned, and the laser should normally lase when switched on. Sometimes during transit or accidentally the laser gets misaligned and hence does not lase. Also when the laser tube is replaced, it is to be aligned. There may be other situations which warrant alignment of the laser. The procedure given below can be followed if enough caution is exercised.

The aim is to make the optic axis (line joining the centers of curvature of the end mirrors) lie along the axis of the laser capillary tube, or to arrange the mirrors normal to the tube axis if Fabry-Perot resonator is used. A cross drawn on a hard card board with a hole of about 1 mm diameter at the intersection and mounted on *x-y-z* translator is an essential component for this purpose and is shown in Fig. A. 1(a). The laser head is mounted on an optical bench and both the end mirrors are carefully removed and stored. The laser is switched on: the tube has the gas discharge. The cross is mounted about 20 cm away from the mirror mount, and the discharge in the capillary tube is seen through the pin-hole. The cross is moved in its plane till the appearance in the field is as shown in Fig. A. 1(c). The outer circular rim corresponds to the near end of the tube and the dot is far end of the tube. When these are concentric, the far end, near end and the pin-hole are in a line: the center of the pin-hole is on the tube axis. The mirror is assembled in its mount. The cross is now illuminated by white light say from a 25 watt lamp, and the image of the cross formed by the mirror is seen through the pin-hole. Usually the appearance will be as shown in Fig. A. 1(d). In rare cases, it may be completely out of view, and hence not seen. The image should be brought in the field of view with the help of adjusting screws on the mount. The adjustment should be continued till the image is centered on the pin-hole like the cross shown in Fig. A. 1(e) This ensures that the tube axis and mirror axis are coincident. This procedure is first done with the output mirror. Therefore, the output mirror is now aligned. No extra care is required for achieving this condition.

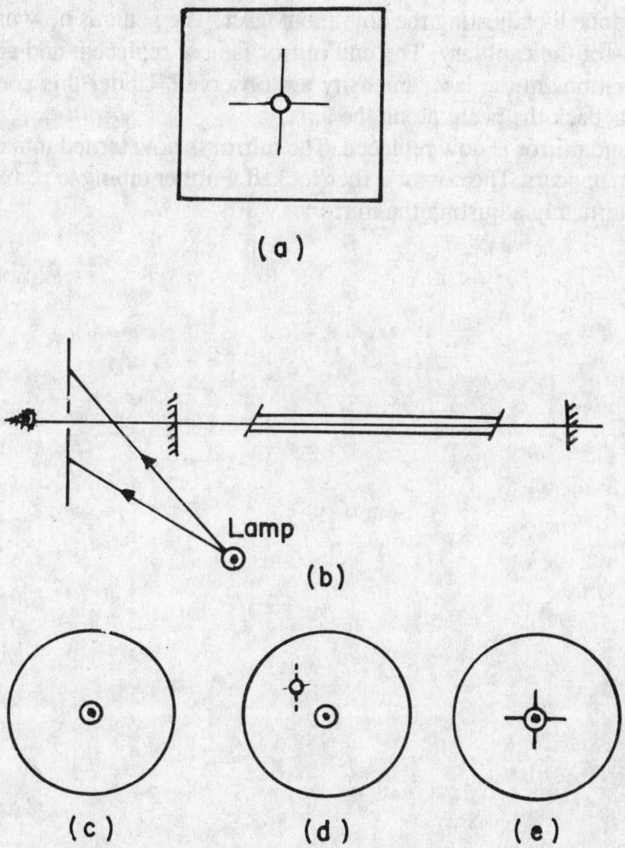


**Fig. A1.** Alignment of Laser: (a) Cross with Viewing Pin-hole, (b) Alignment Setup, (c) Field of View when Pin-hole is on tube Axis, (d) Field of view when Mirror Misaligned and (e) Aligned

The cross is now mounted on the other side of the tube and aligned so that it is on its axis. The mirror is now replaced in its mount and the cross is illuminated by white light. CAVEAT-do not look through the pin-hole unless a paper or any other absorber is placed between the Brewster window and the output mirror. This breaks the optical circuit, and safeguards the eye from accidental laser exposure. The mirror is now aligned following the procedure similar to the one adapted for the output mirror. Now do not look through the pin-hole, and remove the paper to open the optical circuit. The laser should lase now. If the beam does not appear, little turn of the adjustment screws on both the mirrors should restore the lasing. The power output can be peaked by alternately adjusting the mirrors.

For long tube laser (consequently of high power outputs), an auxiliary laser of low power is used. The output mirror of the laser is removed, and the beam from the alignment laser is directed along the tube. The alignment laser is adjusted in its mount such that the beam traverses the capillary without hitting the walls. This can be easily seen by removing the end mirror and looking at the beam on a screen. This alignment is done by adjusting the alignment laser. The beam is now propagating along the axis of the capillary. The end mirror is now replaced, and adjusted till violent fluctuations in the laser intensity are observed. Under this condition the mirror reflects back the beam along the axis.

The near end mirror is now replaced. The mirror is now turned in its mount till the laser beam appears. The mirror is then locked. Further tuning to peak the output is done by alternately adjusting the mirrors.

## Appendix B

# Setting up of a Beam Expander

A beam from a laser is narrow say about 1-2 mm in diameter. For many applications it is to be expanded. A beam expander usually consists of two lenses; one of a small focal length and other of a large focal length. In its adjusted form it is an afocal system: an inverted telescope. For high power lasers, small focal length lens is usually concave. However, with the gas laser it is a microscope objective of 10*X*, 20*X*, or 45*X* magnification depending on the expansion and uniformity of the beam required. At the focal plane of the microscope objective is placed a pin-hole of about 20 μm diameter in a *x-y* mount. The optimum size of the pin-hole is equal to the waist size of the beam at the focal plane of the microscope objective. The objective itself is mounted on a linear stage providing for *z* displacement. The collimator lens is a focal length away from the pin-hole, and has a provision for *z* translation. Figure 1.5 gives a schematic diagram of a beam expander. Initially the microscope objective and pin-hole combination is aligned: The collimator lens is removed. The pin-hole is aligned as follows:

The laser beam is focussed on the pin-hole as seen visually. Care should be exercised while looking at the focussed beam. If the pin-hole is centered on the objective's axis, a weak spot of laser beam may be seen on the screen placed behind the pin hole. The irradiance of this spot is maximised by moving the pin-hole with *x-y* positioner. Now the microscope objective is moved towards the pin-hole. A system of circular rings will be seen. The pin-hole is adjusted such that the brightest spot is in the center of the ring pattern. On further translation the ring pattern will expand, and the bright spot usually will go out of alignment. The spot is again brought to the center of the fringe pattern by translating the pin-hole in its *x-y* stage. This procedure is continued as the objective is translated towards the pin-hole. At one stage, the ring pattern will vanish and the central spot will fill the whole field. This is the correct setting; the beam waist is centrally situated at the pin-hole and the beam is said to be spatially filtered. If the objective is further translated, the ring pattern will reappear. The microscope objective is then withdrawn and procedure repeated.

At the correct setting, the beam is clean. Now the collimator lens is mounted in position. The emerging beam is nearly collimated. A rough method to check the collimation is to observe the beam size at various distances from the collimator lens. The beam should roughly maintain the size. A somewhat better method would be to use a plane mirror to reflect back the beam. An image of the pin-hole will be formed around it. By translating the collimator lens, the image is sharpened. This is a near collimation stage. An interferometric method to check for the collimation in shear interferometry. A plane parallel plate (ppp) is inserted in the beam at an angle, and the interference between the beams reflected from the front and back surfaces of the plate is observed on a screen. Since the plate is positioned at an angle in the beam, the reflected beams are laterally displaced (sheared). Usually one would observe a straight line pattern if the beam is not collimated but is near collimation. The collimator lens is moved along *z* axis (along the beam) such that the number of fringes in the pattern decreases. At one position, there will be only one fringe: the field will be uniformly illuminated. This is the position for collimation. At this position beams reflected from the plate are laterally displaced plane waves with constant path difference over the whole overlap area. Hence, the field is uniformly illuminated. If the collimator lens is further translated, the straight line fringe pattern will reappear.

# Appendix C

# Laser Safety Criterion: Potential Ocular Injury

Concurrent with the development of laser technology, understanding of potential hazards associated with the use of lasers has been expanding. Tentative safe exposure levels and more specific guidelines have been evolved from laser bio-effects studies. The basic concept of the classification schemes of ANSI (American National Standards Institute), ACGIH (American Conference of Government Industrial Hygienists), WHO (World Health Organisation), IEC (International Electrotechnical Commission), and BRH (Bureau of Radiological Health) is as follows:

***Class I:** Class I laser products are essentially safe and are typically enclosed systems which do not emit hazardous levels.

***Class II:** Class II laser products are limited to visible lasers that are safe for momentary viewing but should not be stared at continuously unless the exposure is within the recommended ocular limits.

***Class III:** Class III laser products are not safe even for momentary viewing, and procedural controls and protective equipment are normally required for their use.

***Class IV:** Class IV laser products are normally considered more hazardous than class III devices since they may represent a significant fire hazard or skin hazard and may also produce hazardous diffuse reflection.

The eye is the organ of the body considered the most vulnerable to injury from laser radiation. Hence most considerations of laser hazards concentrate on ocular effects. The main cause of this is that the laser beam can be focused to a very small spot approximately of 10 μm diameter on the retina. The radiant energy per unit area in laser beam incident on the cornea may be increased by million times at the retina. This enormous factor of concentration explains why retinal injury is caused by staring at the laser beam. If the laser beam is viewed after reflection from the diffuse surface, or after transmission through a transluscent material, it becomes an extended source, and hence a large image is formed. Even then the energy concentration is high enough to cause retinal burns. The diffuse reflections are hazardous if the laser operates between 400 nm and 1400 nm. Following table gives the ANSI and BRH classification for He-Ne laser, and ocular exposure limits.

**He-Ne laser CW: λ = 632.8 nm**

| | | |
|---|---|---|
| 1. | BRH and ANSI z–136.1 classifications | Class I if power output <0.4 μW<br>Class II if power output <1 mW<br>Class III if power output <0.5 W<br>Class IV if power output >0.5 W<br>ANSI classification is same except that the upper limit of class I laser power output is 6.5 μW |
| 2. | Ocular exposure limits* | 0.5 μJ/cm² for 1 ns to 18 μs<br>1.8 $t^{3/4}$ mJ/cm² from 18 μs to 450 s<br>170 mJ/cm² from 10 s to $10^4$ s and<br>17 μW/cm² for greater duration |

*The exposure limit is averaged over a 7 mm aperture.

Whenever the exposure exceeds the exposure limits, protective eye-wear should necessarily be used as this provides many orders of magnitude safety. Holographic viewing and optical alignment procedures generally do not require eye wear if reasonable precautions are followed.

The laser laboratory should be brightly illuminated. Raising the ambient light level results in contracting the eye pupil thereby lesser laser energy reaches the retina. Use of less reflective diffuse surface in a bright lit laboratory provides a safety factor of approximately 10. All optical arrangements/layouts should be so configured that the direct laser beam does not rise to the eye-level, and wherever possible, backstops should be positioned to block the laser beam. The laser laboratory should have a caution mark 'EYE HAZARD AREA' displayed prominently. Entry of unauthorised persons in the laboratory should be restricted.

# Suggested Readings


1. Born M. and Wolf E., Principles of Optics, Pergoman Press, New York (1975).
2. Candler, C., Modern Interferometers, Hilger and Watts, London (1951).
3. Cathey, W.T., Optical Information Processing and Holography, Wiley-Interscience, New York (1974).
4. Collier, R.J. Burkhardt, C.B. and Lin, L.H., Optical Holography, Academic Press, New York (1971).
5. Dainty, J.C. (Ed.), Laser Speckle and related Phenomena, Springer Verlag, Berlin (1975).
6. Drain, L.F., The Laser Doppler Technique, Wiley Publication (1980).
7. Fran'con, M., Holography, Academic Press, New York (1974).
8. Fran,con, M., Optical Image Formation and Processing, Academic Press, New York (1979)
9. Francon, M., Laser Speckle and Applications in Optics, Academic Press, New York (1979).
10. Goodmann, J.W., Introduction to Fourier Optics, McGraw-Hill, New York (1968).
11. Heard, H.G., Laser Parameter Measurement Handbook, Wiley, New York (1968).
12. Kallard, T., Exploring Laser Light, Optosonic Press, New York (1977).
13. McAleese, F., The Laser Experiments Handbook, McGraw-Hill, New York (1979).
14. Rogers, G.L., Handbook of gas laser experiments, Illiffee Books Ltd., London (1970).
15. Shulman, A.R., Optical Data Processing, Wiley, New York (1970).
16. Timoshenko, S. and Krieger, S.W., Theory of Plates and Shells, McGraw-Hill, New York (1959).
17. Wright, G. and Foxcroft, G.E., Elementary Experiments with Lasers, Wykham Publications (1973).
18. Lasers and Light, Scientific American (1965).

# Index